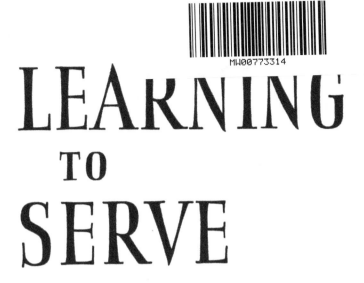

LEARNING
TO
SERVE

A BOOK FOR NEW ALTAR BOYS

by **FATHER CHARLES J. CARMODY**

2015

ST. AUGUSTINE ACADEMY PRESS

HOMER GLEN, ILLINOIS

This book is newly typeset based on the 1961 text
by The Bruce Publishing Company.
All editing strictly limited to the correction of errors
in the original text.

Nihil Obstat:
    ROBERT J. CHISHOLM, *Chancellor*
    Censor librorum
Imprimatur:
    ✠ THOMAS L. NOA
    Bishop of Marquette
    April 4, 1961

This book was originally published in 1961
by The Bruce Publishing Company.

ISBN: 978-1-936639-73-1

All illustrations in this book, including the cover,
are the same illustrations found in the original book.

Contents...

Appendix

Lesson 1 ...

A Catholic Boy's Greatest Honor

To be an altar boy is a great honor—the greatest honor that any Catholic boy can win for himself. But remember, being an altar boy is not easy. It's not just a sideline or something extra for you to do. It's a pretty big job. Before you begin, you should know that being an altar boy is going to demand your interest and a great deal of your time. Remember this too—*serving must always come first*. As time goes on, you will become interested in other things that will also take your time and your interest, but being an altar boy must always be your *first loyalty*. It must never take second place. You must understand this from the beginning.

For these reasons, not just anyone can be an altar boy, but only those boys who make themselves worthy by *prayer, long study*, and *all-round good behavior*. If you are not ready to do all of these things, then you cannot be an altar boy.

This book is going to help you to become a first-class server. The many lessons that follow will teach you what you must know to begin serving. LEARNING TO SERVE will also remind you of what kind of boy you must try to be. It will take a lot of effort to learn the lessons in this book, but *if you have what it takes*, you can do it. Anyone can quit when the going gets tough, but not everyone can see a hard job through to the end. Can you? Well, we shall see.

Always remember, an altar boy must be a *really* good boy. Many years ago in Nazareth, our Lord Himself was once a boy just like you. Put yourself in His place. Try to think and act the way He did. But remember—you are not just putting on a big show. Absolutely not! You must really try to be like our Lord *deep down* inside of yourself. It takes a long time to get ready for the great honor of serving at God's altar. So get busy.

To prepare yourself for the big job ahead, be certain to do three things:

1. Say your prayers as well as you can each day.
2. Go to Holy Communion more often.
3. Always be polite and obedient at home, at school, and in your neighborhood.

If you do these things, you will be on the right road.

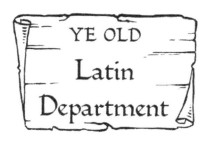

Latin Department

How do you do? Come in. This is the Latin Department. Make yourself at home. You will be in here a lot.

Do you know anything about Latin? Well, Latin is a very old language, and for many years it played a very important part in the history of the world. The Romans used Latin every day, just as we use English. For many hundreds of years, Latin was spoken in many parts of the world. Of course, this is no longer the case. Today, we call Latin a *dead* language, because no nation uses it as an everyday language. We also call Latin a *dead* language because it never changes. A language that is used in everyday speech, like English or German, changes all the time—new words are made up and old words change their meanings.

After all these years, however, the Catholic Church still uses Latin as her official world-wide language. Since Catholics all over the world speak many different languages, it is necessary that we have some language that we can all use together. The Church's language should not be a language that belongs to just one people. It should be a language that belongs to everyone. Besides this, the Church needs a very exact language that doesn't change. Now Latin fills the bill perfectly. Because Latin is a *dead* language, it belongs to everyone. For the same reason, it never changes and is very exact. This is why the Church uses Latin as her official, worldwide language; and, of course, this is why the Mass is in Latin.

One of your chief duties as an altar boy will be to answer the priest at the altar in Latin. Now, even though you do not know Latin, you can still pronounce it correctly if you try. You will see.

To begin with, say these familiar words aloud:

odd	cool	spare	coot	see	key
trees	cheap	lay	tee	rot	lay
flea	may	tar	bear	clay	bee
knee	doom	loom	cot	tote	moose
cone	day	too	you	sock	pair
ill	pool	ten	forty	knee	ark
in	bay	spear	dough	loud	stay
ray	you	me	is	glow	said

Perhaps you did not know it, but you were just making Latin sounds. Even though Latin and English are two different languages, they both use the same sounds, and you know most of these sounds already.

To make it easier for you, your Latin prayers will be written in the English word sounds that you use every day. It's something like the phonics that you use in school. We will write the words, not as they are really spelled in Latin, but as they sound in English. For instance, the Latin word *Deus* means *God*. How would you pronounce it? Well, using English word sounds, it's written like this: **Day-oose**. How would you pronounce it now? The best part of all this is that we can do it with almost any Latin word and get it right.

Remember, now, in your lessons even though you will be reading English word sounds, you will be speaking in Latin. Get the idea?

Things to Know

1. Can just anyone be an altar boy? Explain.
2. What do we mean when we say, "serving should come first"? Is this easy?
3. How does a boy make himself worthy to be a server?
4. Does an altar boy just act like a good boy? Who should an altar boy try to be like?
5. When was Latin used more than it is today? Why does the Church still use Latin?

Things to Do

1. Be able to read all the words on page 8 without a mistake.
2. Be able to tell the name of your book and how many lessons it has.
3. Get a nice plastic bag to carry your book in. Write your name and address on your book.

Lesson 2 ...

The Altar Boy's Ideals

Do you know what this word means—ideals? Well, it means the goals that a person shoots for in his life. *You must have high ideals.* If your ideals are low, you will never be much good. Everyone needs high ideals, especially an altar boy. As we learned the first day, an altar boy must try to be as good as possible. If you pass this course, you will be chosen to serve in your parish sanctuary. This is a great honor and you must be sure that you live up to it. Just as the priest himself, altar boys must be careful to give good example to the rest of the parish. But *remember, remember, remember,* this *doesn't* mean that you are supposed to put on a show and pretend to be something that you are not. It does mean that you must try to be the kind of boy our Lord wants you to be—not just a *goody-goody* or a sissy, but a *good Catholic boy*.

We said that ideals are like goals to shoot for. Almost every game you play has a goal. Can you name some? Well anyway, before you play a game, you have to know *what* the goal is and *where* it is. Boys just don't run around a playing field for nothing; they are shooting for a goal. What would you think of a player who suddenly got the football in the middle of an important game and said, "Hey, what do I do now?" By the time he said it, he would be smothered by the other team. You have to know the goals in a game and you have to know the ideals in being an altar boy.

In the lessons ahead, you will learn all about these ideals. Like any goals, the ideals of an altar boy demand a lot of hard work and trying. So pay close attention to what is expected of you. Don't be like the poor fellow on the football field who didn't know what to do. KNOW YOUR GOALS AND THEN SHOOT FOR THEM WITH ALL YOUR MIGHT.

Latin Department

Well, here we are in the Latin Department again! Are you ready? In the first lesson we learned that Latin and English use the same sounds. Remember? Well, let's take a look now at the most important of these sounds. There are five of them:

1. **ah** sounds—ah as in rah-rah
2. **ay** sounds—ay as in lay
3. **ee** sounds—*ee* as in s*ee*
4. **o**   sounds—o as in no
5. **oo** sounds—*oo* as in m*oo*n

The class must now go over these sounds many times until everyone knows them by heart. These are the sounds of the Latin vowels—a, e, i, o, u. (Notice how **ee** and **oo** are printed—*ee* and *oo*. We will use this special printing all the way through.)

Now that we have seen the five most important sounds, we shall try to put them to work. Ready?

    ah sounds—ah, rah, sah, lah
                ah, kah, wah, kwah
                ah, aht, ahl, ahm

Did you notice how the **ah** sound is always the same? Sometimes, we placed a consonant before the ah and sometimes after the **ah**, making different kinds of **ah** sounds. We shall do the same with the other sounds now.

    ay sounds—ay, lay, say, day, bay
                clay, ray, may, chay (ch as in chair)
    ee sounds—*ee*, s*ee*, f*ee*, n*ee*, m*ee*
                ee, w*ee*, kw*ee*, t*ee*, r*ee*

o sounds—o, no, go, so

o, cone, lone

oo sounds—*oo*, no*o*n, m*oo*n, l*oo*n

l*oo*m, *oo*m, t*oo*, p*oo*l

*oo*se, l*oo*se, c*oo*se, r*oo*m, tr*oo*m

You must go over these sounds again and again. Only practice makes perfect.

Things to Know

1. What are goals? What are ideals? Are they the same? Explain.
2. What is the big thing to remember about goals and ideals?
3. What kind of a boy does our Lord expect you to be?
4. Are altar boys expected to give good example? Why?
5. How can you learn your sounds best?

Things to Do

1. Ask your parents what they think a "good Catholic boy" is.
2. Learn the five most important sounds by heart.
3. Visit your parish church and make a visit to the Blessed Sacrament. While you are there, look around and see how many objects you can name.

Lesson 3 ...

The Altar Boy Does His Very Best

Did you ever notice that you do some things better than others? In school you are good in some subjects but poor in others. You even play some games better than others. The simple reason for this is that some things are easy for you, while other things are pretty hard. This is going to be true all through your life. This is the way that God made you. So, you might as well get used to it.

The only trouble is that most people like to do the easy things but hate to do the hard things. Many people just do the things that they like to do and don't bother with the hard things. These poor people are called the "quitters"—when things get tough, they quit. You can't depend on them. In fact, you might say that they are cowards, always running away from their problems. They never finish anything they start. Always remember, boys, no problem is ever solved by running away from it. Everyone has problems. You just have to face your problems and solve them. You can't be a "quitter."

Our Lord doesn't approve of a "quitter." He certainly wasn't a "quitter" Himself. He faced up to things right to the end. He doesn't want you to be a "quitter" either. Our Lord wants us to do our best in everything. He said so. He wants us to do the easy things perfectly. Remember, not just enough to get by with, but perfectly. What about the things we find hard to do? Our Lord still wants us to do these things as well as we can possibly do them. So don't get discouraged when things get hard to do. Keep your chin up and put your best foot forward. Give the best you've got. This is what our Lord expects of you.

Now, in learning to become an altar boy, some things will be easy for you—other things will be hard. So make up your mind right now to do the easy things perfectly and the hard things just as well as you can. Another thing—those in charge of your training will correct you many, many times. Don't pout when you are corrected or go over in the corner and feel sorry for yourself. *You need to be corrected—everybody does.* Pay attention to the corrections and put them into practice. Don't let them go into one ear and out the other. Above all, don't be a "quitter." REMEMBER YOU WILL NEVER, NEVER DO A GOOD JOB IF YOU CAN'T TAKE CORRECTION. So get ready—you're going to get a lot of it. That's it, boys—stick to it. Don't be a "quitter." Put your best foot forward and go to it.

Latin Department

Hello! Did you learn your five sounds? The five Latin sounds that we learned in the last lesson are so important that we must go over them again. Let each boy show the class how well he has learned them:

ah is pronounced _____   **ee** is pronounced _____

ay is pronounced _____   **o** is pronounced _____

oo is pronounced _____

Now besides the ah, ay, *ee*, and *oo* sounds, Latin has four other important sounds. Here they are:

air sounds—chair, tair, vair, sair
aw sounds—saw, daw, naw, taw
ez sounds—fez, rez, ez, tez
en sounds—ten, men, en, sen, ven

There are nine important sounds then. These nine sounds must be known perfectly and by heart. So be certain to have all nine sounds ready for the next class.

Things to Know

1. Why do we do some things better than others?
2. Who are the "quitters"? Explain.
3. Does everyone have problems? How do we solve them?
4. What does our Lord want us to do?
5. Who needs to be corrected? How should we take correction?

Things to Do

1. Keep reviewing the first five sounds over and over again.
2. Learn the second four sounds by heart.
3. Find out what your school principal thinks of "quitters."

Lesson 4 ...

The Altar Boy Knows His Rubrics

You have heard many times that the Catholic Church is the same all over the world. No matter where you go, Catholics believe the same things, have the very same Mass and Sacraments, and all obey the Holy Father in Rome. But it's important to remember that in different parts of the world, Catholics offer the same Holy Mass in many different ways. It all depends on what *rite* you belong to. In the Catholic Church there are a number of different *rites*. Each *rite* has its own language and official way of praying, which we call *liturgy*. This is a good word for you to remember—*liturgy*. Most Catholics, including us, belong to the *Roman Rite*. We use Latin in the Mass and other services. Many other Catholics, however, belong to what we call *Eastern Rites*. They use Greek or some other language. Each rite has its own official prayer books written in its own language. We have five official prayer books and they are written in Latin.

All these official prayer books are printed in two colors—black and red. The *prayers* are printed in black, but the rules that tell us what to do are printed in *red letters*. Now the Latin word for red letters is *rubrica*. Because the rules for serving are printed in red letters, they are also called *rubrica*. In English we use almost the same word, but we change the final "a" to an "s" and get *rubrics*. There it is. That's the word you have to know. *Rubrics. Rubrics. Rubrics. Rubrics* are the rules for serving. *Rubrics* tell us when to stand, sit, kneel, turn around, bow, and a lot of other things.

Part of your job as an altar boy will be to learn the *rubrics* or rules for serving Mass and other services. But, get this straight from the start. You don't just make it up as you go along or wander around the altar like a wild buffalo. No indeed, you are supposed to serve according to the *rubrics*. What's the word—everybody? That's right, the *rubrics*.

Latin Department

Greetings, come into the Latin Department. Well, you found out that you all belong to the Roman Rite, and the Roman Rite uses Latin as its official language. So, you can see that we're on the right track here.

In the last few lessons, we learned nine important

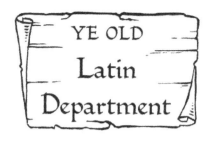

YE OLD
Latin
Department

Latin sounds.   Now once more, let's go over them again. Each boy must have these sounds at his finger tips. Let's go over the sounds together a few times. Here they are:

ah ____	ay ____	ee ____
o ____	oo ____	air ____
aw ____	ez ____	en ____

Now that we have a pretty fair idea of the most important sounds, let's put them to work for ourselves. On one side, you will find the Latin word; and on the other side, the same word written in English word sounds. Ready?

Latin words	English word sounds
Pater	**pah-tair**
Petrum	**pay-tr**oo**m**
repulisti	**ray-p**oo**l-is-t**ee
aeternam	**ay-tair-nahm**
terram	**tair-ahm**

These are some of the words that cause trouble. So if you learn them now, it will help you later on.

Things to Know

1. What is the Roman Rite? How many different rites are there?
2. Do you know what the word "liturgy" means? Explain.
3. What are "rubrics"? Where does the word come from?
4. Are rubrics important? What would happen if we didn't have rubrics?
5. What language does the Roman Rite use? What can you tell about the Church's language?

Things to Do

1. Have the nine most important sounds at your finger tips.
2. Be able to name the other Catholic churches in your city or deanery. Are they all of the Roman Rite?
3. Be able to tell your bishop's full name and the full name of your pastor and other parish priests too. Can you find a picture of your bishop? Do you have a picture of the Holy Father?

Lesson 5 ...

The Altar Boy Knows Himself

No one is perfect. It's too bad, but it's true. We are all a bundle of strong points and weak points. Did you know that? Well, ever since our first parents, Adam and Eve, committed original sin it's been that way. Since that time, we all have a hard time controlling ourselves. The strong points and weak points are always fighting to see which will get the upper hand. Which will win? Well, it's up to us. Will we turn out to be strong or weak? It depends on which set of points gets control. Just what are your strong points? What are your weak points? Do you know? You should.

Many hundreds of years ago, a great and wise man named Socrates said, "Know yourself." He was right, too.

We can never control ourselves unless we understand our strong points and our weak points. With our Lord's help, we can improve ourselves; but first, we must find out where we need the improving.

In the clays ahead, study yourself very well. See if you can pick out your strong points and weak points. Ask your parents and teachers to help you. Sometimes, they know you better than you know yourself. At any rate, see if you can figure yourself out.

GOOD NEWS

Latin Department

Good news. Today we are ready to learn the first Latin responses that you will use at Mass. They are called responses because they are your answers to the priest's prayers. As you remember, the Mass opens with the priest and servers saying the Prayers at the Foot of the Altar. Here is the first one of these responses. Who can read it right off?

Ahd Day'-*oo*m kw*ee* lay-t*ee*'-f*ee*-kaht/ y*oo*-ven-t*oo*'-tem may'-ahm.

There it is—the first response (answer). You have often heard that practice makes perfect, and this is very true. IT IS ONLY BY GOING OVER THESE PRAYERS AGAIN AND AGAIN THAT YOU WILL LEARN THEM.

Now, two last things. You know that words are made up of parts called *syllables*. One of the syllables is hit by your voice. We call this the *accent*. Notice now that where the mark ' appears at the end of a syllable. This is where the accent is placed. Hit that one syllable when you say the word. Another thing, too, when you see the mark / pause there before going on—not too long though.

Today's Rubrics

Now that we know what the rubrics are, we can begin to study them. In each lesson, we will study a new rubric. By the time you have finished with LEARNING TO SERVE, you will know all of the most important rubrics. Some of the Church's ceremonies are very simple; others are very difficult; but *in every ceremony, no matter how simple or how difficult, we use the same rubrics.*

Today, we shall look over some of the official prayer books of the Roman Rite where the rubrics are written down in red letters. Here they are:

Roman Missal—This is the large book used at Mass. Besides the big missal which contains everything, there is also a smaller missal which contains only the Masses for the dead. There is also a special missal for use in Holy Week. The bishop also has a special book for use at Mass called the *Canon*.

Roman Breviary—This is the Church's daily prayer book. It contains the Divine Office. You have often seen the priest with his office book or breviary.

Roman Ritual—This book contains the Church's blessings and the ceremonies for the Sacraments.

Roman Pontifical—This is a special book used by the bishop. It contains the ritual for Confirmation, Holy Orders, etc.

Ceremonial of Bishops—This is another very special book for the use of the bishop.

These then are most of the official prayer books of the Roman Rite. You should remember at least the first three.

Things to Know

1. Who said, "Know thyself"? What does it mean? Explain.
2. What are "responses"? Are "responses" prayers?
3. How can you learn your Latin prayers best?
4. What is a "syllable"? What is an "accent"?
5. Name some of the official prayer books of the Roman Rite.

Things to Do

1. Make a list of your strong points and weak points. Ask your parents and teachers to help you make your list.
2. Keep reading over your first response until you can read it without a mistake.
3. Say a special prayer tonight that God will help you be a good and faithful altar boy.

Lesson 6 ...

The Altar Boy Recites His Latin Correctly, Clearly, and With Certainty

To recite his Latin correctly and clearly, an altar boy must learn to *articulate* and to *project* his voice. Pretty big words, aren't they? Well, let's take them one at a time.

Articulate—say it together. Ready? Ar-ti′-cu-late. This word means that when you speak you use *all* of your speaking equipment. God gave you a tongue, lips, teeth, and a palate to speak with. If you don't *articulate* or use all of this speaking equipment, you will never speak correctly. Instead, you will swallow your words, mumble them, or slur over them, and you will not be understood. Sometimes, it is necessary to exaggerate or to overspeak to get into the habit of *articulating*. This is especially true when speaking Latin. In Latin the endings of the words are very important. So remember, be careful to speak each Latin word slowly and exactly. You must learn to *articulate—articulate—articulate*.

An altar boy must also *project* his voice. This means that he must speak out loudly and clearly, but without shouting. To do this, you must breathe properly. You must learn to breathe from the lungs, as all great singers and speakers do. When you are in bed tonight, lie on your back and notice how slowly, evenly, and deeply you are breathing. This is the proper way to breathe.

So remember, an altar boy must *articulate* and *project* his voice. He answers for all the people at Mass. His Latin responses must be made *correctly, clearly,* and *with certainty*. During the Mass, the priest uses two tones of voice. When the server makes his responses, he should be careful to use the same tone of voice that the priest is then using. Ordinarily, the people kneeling in the church should be able to hear the altar boy's responses. If the server articulates and projects his voice properly, he will be heard without shouting. So please, no swallowing of words, no mumbling, no slurring. Learn to *articulate*— use all of your speaking equipment. Learn to *project* your voice. For goodness' sakes, don't be a mumbler.

Latin Department

Hello! Did every boy learn the first response (answer)? If so, we can go on to the second response. Remember, you have to keep going over these prayers again and again. This is a long one, and so, you probably cannot learn it in just one class.

Kwee**'-ah t**oo **ez Day'-**oos**/**
for-tee**-t**oo**'-doe may'-ah/**
kwah'-ray may ray-poo**l-is'-t**ee**/**
et kwah'-ray tree**s'-tis in-chay'-doe/**
doo**m ah-fl**ee**'-ghit may in-**ee**-m**ee**'-k**oo**s.**

Each boy should be careful to observe the pauses marked with /. By the way, boys always seem to have difficulty in the third line of the response because there are three **ay** sounds in a row. Be careful that you get all three of them in. Practice makes perfect.

Today's Rubrics

You have seen the priest in different colored vestments many times. Do you know how many colors the Church uses? Well, there are five. Here are a few things for you to remember about them:

White—used in Masses of our Lord, the Blessed Mother, and saints who are not martyrs.

Red—used in Masses of martyrs and the Holy Ghost.

Green—used on most Sundays of the year (Sundays after Pentecost).

Violet—used in Lent and Advent and Masses of Penance.

Black—used in Masses for the dead.

There are three other colors that may be used at times:

Rose—may be used on the third Sunday of Advent and the fourth Sunday of Lent.

Gold—may be used in place of white, green, or red. The vestments must be made of gold wire and not gold-colored cloth.

Silver—may be used in place of white only. Silver vestments must be made from silver wire.

The color *blue* is used at certain shrines of the Blessed Virgin in Spain.

Things to Know

1. What do we mean by the words "to articulate" and "to project the voice"?
2. How does a first-class server make his responses?
3. Name the five colors the Church uses in the liturgy.
4. Be able to name some other colors the Church sometimes uses.

Things to Do

1. Be able to tell what color vestments the priest wore last Sunday and during this week.
2. Ask two of your neighbors to write letters of recommendation for you, proving that you will be a credit to your parish as an altar boy.
3. Review your first response. Keep reading over the response for this lesson until you can read it without a mistake.

Lesson 7...

The Altar Boy Is a Christian Gentleman

We use the term gentleman pretty freely nowadays. Everyone gets called a gentleman, but not everyone is a gentleman—far from it. Do you know what a gentleman is? Well, he is a kind and gentle person who tries to be good and kind to other people. A gentleman respects other people, their property, their feelings, and their good name.

Now, our Lord wants all of us to be gentlemen— Christian gentlemen. He wants us to be good to one another and get along with one another as well as we can. It isn't easy though —is it? We often talk back, have loud arguments, and sometimes real fights. Besides, we all know some fellows who get us mad just to look at them.

Well, no one is perfect and we all get on each other's nerves once in a while; but the important thing is to try to get along and help one another in spite of it. Keep this in the back of your mind: our Lord wants me to be a gentleman—a Christian gentleman. He wants me to respect other people, their property, their feelings, and their good name.

A gentleman tries to be very careful about teasing other fellows or poking fun at them. Sometimes, we do more harm than we realize. Maybe some boys have big ears or funny teeth. Some boys are taller than we are, or shorter, or heavier, or maybe they stutter, or wear glasses, or can't run very fast. Is this any reason to tease them and make them feel foolish? After all, take a good look in the mirror sometime—maybe you look funny to some people, too. Besides, if someone is different than you are, that's his business, not yours. So mind your own business. You have enough wrong with yourself without making fun of other people. Some boys can be very cruel and mean without knowing it. Trying to be funny, they hurt other people's feelings and cause them a lot of sorrow. So be kind to each other. This is what our Lord wants. He wants you to be a gentleman—a Christian gentleman. See that you make yourself just that—a Christian gentleman.

Latin Department

Come in, boys. Here we are in *Lesson 7* already. Well, you know the second part of the next response. So this one should be easy for you.

**Et in-tro-*ee'*-bo ahd ahl-tah'-ray Day'-*ee*/
ahd Day'-*oo*m kw*ee* lay-t*ee'*-f*ee*-kaht/
y*oo*-ven-t*oo'*-tem may'-ahm.**

Remember, the **o** sounds in these responses are pronounced as o in no. Be careful in the **oo** sounds to give nice round **oo**'s. Make sure that you keep repeating the responses we learn over and over until you have them down perfectly. Remember, the first-class server makes his Latin responses correctly, clearly, and with certainty.

Today's Rubrics

The difference between a good altar boy and a scarecrow is his *stance*. Likewise, the difference between a good altar boy and a yo-yo is his *stance*. This simply means that an altar boy doesn't stand stiff like a scarecrow or doesn't bob up and down like a yo-yo. The altar boy has a definite position which is called his *stance*. YOU CAN ALWAYS TELL A WELL-TRAINED SERVER BY HIS STANCE.

Here is the stance—your position of attention:

Head—the head is kept straight, with the eyes lowered.

Body—the body is held erect and the shoulders thrown back.

Feet—the feet are kept together, except when in motion.

Hands—the palms and fingers are joined to a point before the breast. They are pointed out.

Be careful not to have the hands too high or too low. Don't let them droop and don't put them near your mouth. Always keep the fingers fully extended and joined; never fold them one over the other; never interlock them. The right thumb should be over the left thumb. A good server always keeps his hands in the correct position.

After each boy has learned the proper stance, he should practice walking. WALK SLOWLY AND EVENLY. Don't wobble like Barnacle Bill the Sailor. Remember, head up, eyes down, shoulders back, hands in place, and slow, even steps.

Things to Know

1. What is a gentleman? What does our Lord expect of us?
2. How can an altar boy be a Christian gentleman? Discuss fully.
3. Sometimes we can be cruel and mean without knowing it. Explain.
4. What is the altar boy's "stance"?
5. What special points must an altar boy remember about his hands?
6. How can you tell a well-trained server? List his qualities.

Things to Do

1. Be able to show the proper stance of an altar boy.
2. Be able to articulate your full name, address, telephone number, and the name of your school and parish.
3. Be able to read the first three responses without a mistake.

Lesson 8...

The Altar Boy Is Respected by His Teachers and Neighbors

We have spoken a good deal about being a gentleman and about doing your work. Well, school is a marvelous place to do it in. Certainly an altar boy should be a leader in his class. He doesn't have to be the smartest boy, but he should be one of the *best behaved* and *most willing* boys in the class. His character grades should always be high. No boy with low character grades should be permitted to serve on the altar. In fact, any boy that is always in trouble with his teachers does not deserve the honor of being a server. Your teachers have a very thankless job. They must educate you and hold you to your duty. For this reason, they are not very popular. It is a strange thing, but we don't always like the people who do the most good for us.

This is also true in your neighborhood. An altar boy should have a good reputation on his block. He doesn't have to be perfect, but his neighbors should agree that he is a good boy and not a rough, sassy, or bold boy. A boy who serves in God's sanctuary should have great respect for other people's property and privacy. Needless to say, an altar boy should never have to be corrected by the police. Don't dishonor your cassock and surplice by being a sorrow to other people. Be sure to co-operate with your teachers and neighbors.

BUT REMEMBER, BOYS, IN ALL OF THIS DON'T BE A HYPOCRITE. PLEASE DON'T PUT ON AN ACT. DON'T JUST *SEEM* TO BE A GOOD BOY—*BE* A GOOD BOY.

Latin Department

Come in. Let's get busy. We have a pretty long response to learn here today. The funny thing is that most boys learn it quite easily. Will you? Here it is:

> **Spay'-rah in Day'-o/**
> **kwo'-n*ee*-ahm ahd'-h*oo*k/**
> **cone-f*ee*-tay'-bor ill'-*ee*/**
> **sah-l*oo*-tah'-ray v*oo*l'-t*oo*s may'-*ee*/**
> **et Day'-*oo*s may'-*oo*s.**

Today's Rubrics

The altar boy must be very careful about the Sign of the Cross. It is used in almost every ceremony. You

1	2	3	4
IN THE NAME OF THE **FATHER,**	AND OF THE **SON,**	AND OF THE **HOLY**	**GHOST, AMEN.**

have been making the Sign of the Cross for many years, but many of you do not make it correctly. You make it carelessly, not fully enough, or much too quickly. Remember, the Sign of the Cross is a prayer. Make it well.

To make the Sign of the Cross properly, do this:

a) Disjoin the hands from their folded position.

b) Place the left hand fully extended just under your breast. Keep the fingers and thumb together.

c) Keep the right fingers fully extended. Place your thumb in the palm.

d) Now slowly trace the Sign of the Cross in broad full strokes. Be careful not to bring the right hand below the left in the second stroke. Be careful to touch the end of each shoulder in the third and fourth strokes.

e) After you have finished, rejoin the hands in front of your breast.

Each boy should practice making the Sign of the Cross correctly. Sometimes it is better to count the strokes than to say the words in practicing the correct way. Like this:

1

3   **4**

2

Things to Know

1. What do we mean when we say the altar boy must be a leader in his class?
2. Do we always like the people who do the most good for us? Explain.
3. How should an altar boy behave in his neighborhood? Why is this important?
4. Many people make the Sign of the Cross incorrectly. Explain.
5. How often do we make the Sign of the Cross? What points should we keep in mind about making the Sign of the Cross?

Things to Do

1. Pick out a good large minor at home in front of which you can practice. Be certain to ask if you may use it.
2. Practice making the Sign of the Cross before your mirror slowly and carefully.
3. Keep reviewing your responses. Pay special attention to the one in this lesson.

Lesson 9...

The Altar Boy Shows Respect to His Superiors at All Times

The next time you see a baby, notice how helpless he is. A baby really can't do anything for himself except make a lot of noise. Everyone has to wait on a baby. You were just like that once too; and if you really want to be honest with yourself, you must admit that in many ways you still depend on others. Often someone else has to do something for you. Just think what a terrible world this would be if God didn't have our mothers and fathers and a whole lot of other people waiting to help us. We would never get along.

We depend on our families to feed us, clothe us, give us a home. We need the priests and the Sisters to help us lead good lives and save our souls. We need our teachers in school to educate us. We need the police, the firemen, the postmen, our family doctors, and so many people to help us. The funny thing is that many times we act very shamefully to these people who help us.

Remember, every time you have food on the table or a new pair of shoes or money in your pocket—it is because your father went out and earned it for you. Every time you have clean clothes and nice meals, and a lot of love and attention—you have your mother to thank for it. You can read and write and do a lot of other things because your teachers in school spent so much time and patience to teach you. Do you ever thank them? Probably you complain that you don't like school and that it's too hard. When are you going to wake up? Without all the help you get from your family, friends, teachers, and a whole lot of other people, you would never be able to grow up. We should all be very grateful to these good people who work so hard to help us. Show your gratitude by being obedient and polite. Co-operate at all times. You will never be able to repay your parents, the Sisters and priests, your teachers, the police, and all the others who have done so much for you. The least that you can do is not to increase their troubles by becoming a problem. Save the back talk too. They don't need it. If suddenly you didn't have all of these good people to help you and train you, how far do you think you would get?

Be grateful to your parents especially, because they are your most loyal friends.

Latin Department

My, most of you are doing pretty well. Keep up the good work. Go over your Latin again and again. Here is the next response. Go to it:

See**'-koot ay'-raht in prin-ch**ee**'-p**ee**-o/
et n**oo**nk et sem'-pair/
et in say'-k**oo**-lah say-k**oo**-lo'-r**oo**m. Amen.**

Notice where the accent is in **ay'-raht**—it's not **ay-raht'**. Also notice the accent in **say'-k**oo**-lah**. By the way, do you study LEARNING TO SERVE at home every night?

Today's Rubrics

In this lesson, we shall learn how to bow and genuflect correctly. These are very important rubrics.

In general, the server should know three kinds of bows:

a) Head bow—only the head is bowed. The shoulders are not moved. *Be careful not to jerk the head.*

b) Shoulder bow—both the head and shoulders are bowed slightly. Not too deeply, but slowly.

c) Deep bow—also called the profound bow. It is made from the waist. If your hands were not joined before your breast, they would touch the knees in this bow.

Single genuflection   Double genuflection

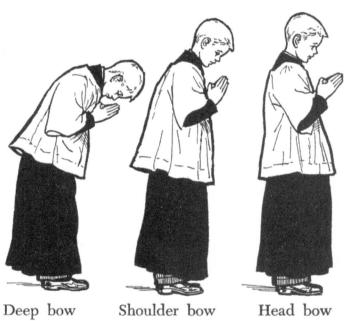

Deep bow   Shoulder bow   Head bow

The genuflection is even more important than the bow. It should be learned correctly from the beginning. There are two kinds of genuflections—the *single* and the *double*. The *single* is made with one knee and the *double* with two knees, plus a deep bow. Some boys have a lot of trouble in genuflecting, so be careful.

The *single genuflection* is the most common of the two. When genuflecting, keep these points in mind:

a) Keep the body and head erect.
b) Keep the hands in place.
c) Slowly bend the right knee to the floor. The knee should reach a position opposite the left heel.
d) After the knee touches the floor, slowly, but immediately rise and take your stance.
e) In all genuflections, go straight down and straight up. Don't *jack-knife*. Don't pop up and down. Don't place your hands on your knee, and, above all, don't wobble.

The *double genuflection* is made by slowly kneeling on both knees (first the right and then the left) and slowly making a shoulder bow. When this is finished, rise and take the proper stance. Remember, it's always done slowly and evenly. Some boys look like they're falling apart when they make a double genuflection. Sometimes the server is called upon to genuflect while standing on a step. This requires some care. However, remember that the genuflection should be made on the step on which you are standing. That means your knee should touch that step and not the step above.

Things to Know

1. How many things can you do for yourself? Make a list.
2. Why do we need older people to help us? What do they do for us?
3. Can we ever really repay our parents and others who help us to grow up? What can we do?
4. How many kinds of bows should a server know how to perform?
5. What points should we remember about the genuflection?

Things to Do

1. Practice making the three bows before your mirror. Remember not to jerk the head.
2. Practice making both kinds of genuflection carefully. Remember to make a deep bow with the double genuflection.
3. Pay special attention to the response of this lesson. Watch the accent on **ay'-raht** and **say'-k**oo-**lah**.

Lesson 10...

The Altar Boy Is Polite and Courteous to Everyone

We talked of respect in the last lesson. Well, very often we show our respect for a person by being polite. Politeness means giving people the respect and reverence they deserve. We can be very free and easy with our friends and playmates, but we should be polite with older people. You and your friends are very close. You are equals. It's all right to say "hi" to them, and even "yah" and "okay." You can even kid them along and poke a little harmless fun at them. This is fine with your friends and equals, but don't try this with your parents, teachers, and older people. It isn't proper. When speaking to them, you must be very polite. To

44

them, it must always be—"yes, sir; no, sir; no, ma'am; yes, ma'am; good morning, Father; good afternoon, Sister; hello, Mr. Smith; yes, Mrs. Jones." Such words as "thank you—please—I beg your pardon—excuse me" should always be found in your everyday language with older people. NEVER BE SHORT OR FAMILIAR WITH OLDER PEOPLE, ESPECIALLY THOSE WHO HAVE CHARGE OF YOU. YOU ARE NOT EQUAL TO THEM, SO DON'T ACT AS IF YOU ARE.

Finally, be very careful of joking with older people. They may joke with you, but be careful about joking back. Sometimes, young boys don't know how to joke with older people and they say things that should not be said. If you don't want to put your foot in your mouth, be careful how you joke with those above you.

One last thing, always greet the priests, Brothers, or Sisters when you see them. Always tip your hat and say hello even if you don't know them personally. They have given up their families and their friends for us. It is only right for us to be friendly and respectful to them. It is a mark of a real Catholic boy always to greet God's servants wherever he meets them.

Latin Department

Greetings! We have two responses in this lesson, but one of them is an old friend. It would be nice if you could know all of your responses as well as you know this one:

Ahd Day'-oo**m kw**ee **lay-t**ee**'-f**ee**-kaht/ y**oo**-ven-t**oo**'-tem may'-ahm.**

The next one is short but some boys have difficulty with it:

Kwee **fay'-chit chay'-l**oo**m et tair'-ahm.**

Notice the **ch** sounds are pronounced as **ch** in chair. That word **tair'-ahm** causes trouble. Please notice that it is **tair'-ahm**, not **tair'-nahm**.

Today's Rubrics

Rising, sitting, and kneeling are three different movements. Some altar boys think that the three are all one. They slide up and slide down. In fact, they look like the cowboy's "tumbling tumbleweed." Rising, sitting, and kneeling all must be done separately. If you remember this, you will never pop up or collapse. You will never take off from a genuflection like a jet rocket and you will never come sliding into your kneeling place looking like "Kelly" sliding for home base. Finally, when

sitting you must never slide off or back up onto the bench. Each time you must rise and stand before you sit or kneel. Remember, too, when seated your hands fully extended should be placed flat on the thighs.

Going up and down steps is a problem, too. Watch where you are going, especially if you are carrying something. Sometimes, your cassock gets tangled up in your feet when you go to get up. *Be sure to remove your cassock from your shoes before you stand.* In fact, be careful that your cassock is not too long. Otherwise, you will have a great deal of trouble with it.

Things to Know

1. What is the difference in the way we speak to our friends and to older people?
2. Why should we be careful about joking with older people?
3. What should Catholics do when they see a priest, a Sister, a Brother? Why?
4. How does an altar boy rise, sit, and kneel? Explain.
5. What should you remember about your cassock when you serve?

Things to Do

1. Practice rising, sitting, and kneeling at home.
2. When you see your pastor, ask him what he thinks an altar boy should be like.
3. Learn your response **Kw**ee **fay'-chit**. Then spend the rest of the time reviewing ones you have already been taught.

47

Lesson 11...

The Altar Boy Is Always in Plenty of Time

If there is one thing that the altar boy must watch, it is being prompt. This doesn't mean just being on time— it means being in *plenty of time*. You can't wait until the last minute and then expect to do a good job. You don't have to camp in the sacristy the night before, but be there at least 15 to 20 minutes before the service. In this way, you will have plenty of time to get vested and get things ready. To get vested, prepare the altar, fix the wine and water, and light the candles takes a good deal of time. See that you have it.

You should time yourself. See how long it takes you to get ready at home. Then see how long it takes you to get from your home to church. It will always take a little longer in bad weather. With this important information, you will be able to plan on just how much time you need to be prompt.

History is full of many important things that happened because one man was late, or one man fell asleep, or one man forgot to give a signal on time. So remember, it is important to be *where* you are supposed to be *when* you are supposed to be there. DON'T JUST BE ON TIME. BE IN PLENTY OF TIME.

Latin Department

Well, today we begin a rather long response. We are still on the Prayers at the Foot of the Altar. They reach their highest point in the *Confiteor*, which is said by the priest first and then by the servers. After the priest has prayed his *Confiteor*, the server answers with this prayer. Let's read it through slowly:

> **M***ee***-say-ray-ah'-t***oor* **t***oo***'-***ee***/**
> **ohm-n***ee***'-po-tens Day'-***oos***/**
> **et d***ee***-m***ee***'-sis pay-kah'-tis t***oo***'-is/**
> **pair-d***oo***'-kaht tay/**
> **odd v***ee***'-tahm ay-tair'-nahm.**

Watch the word **ohm-n***ee***'-po-tens**. Be careful of this one. It's easy to get it mixed up with another word just like it later on.

Today's Rubrics

One of the altar boy's ideals is that he knows his rubrics. The good server not only knows his rubrics

but is careful never to get careless with them. When a server performs his rubrics correctly and smoothly, we say he has good "altar-presence." Altar presence is what separates good servers from poor ones. If you have a big mirror at home, practice in front of it. Don't let yourself get rusty. You must always check up on yourself to keep your rubrics fresh and exact.

Now that we know many of the simple rubrics, the time has come for the whole class to practice them together. We call this group action —that is, action done by the whole group. Remember, when two or more of you serve together, you serve as a group. You must be careful that all your actions and rubrics are done together.

Let's line up now two by two. If possible, every boy should have a partner. Partners should be about the same height. When you are given your partner and place in line, keep it. When the call *Fall in* is given, you and your partner should meet in the place assigned.

When you are lined up in order, you form a *procession*. Remember, when in procession, you are *on parade*. Your main duty is to look dignified and prayerful. You are there to add beauty to the ceremony. Be certain to walk with *head erect, eyes cast down,* and *hands properly joined*. Always walk evenly with your own partner. Keep directly in back of the boy in front of you and stay at least one arm's length behind him. When you turn, make a square turn.

At solemn ceremonies, listen for the signals and perform all of your actions together. When sitting in the pews or in the sanctuary, be careful not to slouch or grow careless. Don't gawk around. Rise, stand, and sit as you have been instructed to do. Good altar-presence is very important in procession.

The altar boy can have a regular *manual of arms*. It goes like this:

Attention—Immediately stop whatever you are doing and listen.

Fall in—You take your place in procession.

Take stance—You take the proper *position of attention*.

Single genuflection
Double genuflection
Sign of the Cross
Head bow
Shoulder bow
Deep bow
Process
Right turn
Left turn
Halt
Fall out
(Other commands may be added.)

If you practice this manual of arms often, your rubrics will be perfect, and you will improve your altar-presence.

Things to Know

1. What does "being prompt" mean to an altar boy?
2. How long before the service should the altar boy arrive? Why?
3. What is "altar-presence"? What is "group action"?
4. How can a server keep his rubrics fresh and exact?
5. How should an altar boy march in procession?

Things to Do

1. Be able to give the server's *manual of arms*.
2. Time yourself to see how long it takes you to get ready in the morning. How long does it take you to walk to church from your house?
3. Read over the **M**ee-**say-ray-ah'-t**oor again and again until you can read it smoothly and without mistakes.

Lesson 12 ...

The Altar Boy Is Responsible for His Altar Appointments

Have you ever heard the expression, "Joe is responsible for it"? Well, this means that Joe must answer for it. The job is his—no one else's. It's on his shoulders and he is the one who must do it.

Responsibility is a big word but it has a simple meaning. It means this—know what your job is and then do it. An altar boy must be a very responsible person. He must know his job and then do it. No one else should have to do it for him.

When an altar boy is assigned to serve, he receives his "altar appointment." When you are given an altar appointment, the church depends on you to be there. You are responsible for it. It's your job. The appointment is on your shoulders. You must answer for it. To help yourself, be sure that you know exactly when you are appointed to serve. Even though your family should be interested in your serving, don't depend on Mother and Dad to remind you. Remember your altar appointments yourself. Why? Well, simply because it's your job and not theirs. You are responsible for it. A little rain or snow shouldn't bother you either. After all, you aren't a cream puff, are you? In very bad weather, your family should arrange for you to get to church and help you keep your appointments. But otherwise, try to keep your appointments on your own. If, for some reason, you cannot keep one of your altar appointments, give yourself plenty of time to get a proper substitute. A proper substitute means a boy of your own height and ability. In emergencies, altar boys should be ready to serve for one another on short notice. An altar boy's family should help him get to church on time for such emergencies. If, in an emergency, you cannot get a proper substitute, phone the rectory and report that you cannot take your appointment. Such a situation should be very rare, however. REMEMBER—BE RESPONSIBLE—KNOW YOUR JOB AND THEN DO IT.

Latin Department

Come in and settle down. You are in for a long session. If you can say all the responses we have had so far smoothly and with no mistakes, you are ready to go on to the longest prayer of all—the *Confiteor*. It is divided into five parts for you to learn more easily. Many of you know this *Confiteor* in English. Who can say it in English without a mistake? Well, here is the first part in Latin:

Cone-f*ee*'**-tay-or Day'-o ohm-n***ee***-po-ten'-t***ee***/
bay-ah'-tay mah-r*ee*'**-ay sem-pair v***ee***r'-g***ee***-n***ee***/

Be careful of the **o** sounds. Keep the **o** nice and oval as **o** in note. Please remember to keep reviewing your Latin over and over again. Only practice makes perfect.

Today's Rubrics

Candles are a very important part of our liturgy (who remembers that word?). They remind us of our Lord who is the Light of the World. You can't get along in the darkness without light and you can't get along in your life without our Lord.

In all ceremonies, the Church uses candles made chiefly of beeswax, but not always the same number of candles. Here are some rules for you to learn:

Number of Candles

> *Two candles for a low Mass* (sometimes four, if the Mass is for some special occasion or offered by a bishop)
>
> *Six candles for a high Mass*
>
> *Twelve or more candles for Benediction*
>
> *Twenty candles for 40 Hours' Devotion*

(From Easter to Ascension Thursday, the large paschal candle is also lighted during the Sunday Masses and very often the weekday Masses in most churches. However, the paschal candle is never lighted during a Mass offered in violet or black vestments. In some churches a special candle, called a *Sanctus candle,* is lighted before the Consecration of a low Mass and is extinguished after the Communion. It is usually placed in a wall bracket on the Epistle side.)

Rules for Lighting the Candles

> *The Epistle side is always lighted first* (if a server lights alone).
>
> *The top row is always lighted before the bottom row.*
>
> *In any row the candle next to the tabernacle is lighted first.*

Rules for Extinguishing the Candles

Candles are extinguished backward; that is, just the opposite of the way in which they were lighted.
The last candle lighted is the first one to be put out.
The first candle lighted is the last one to be put out.

We shall hear more about lighting and extinguishing candles in another lesson. In the meantime, learn the rules given above.

Things to Know

1. What does "responsibility" mean? Explain fully.
2. What is an "altar appointment"? How should a server accept his altar appointments?
3. How can you make sure to keep your altar appointments?
4. What is a "proper substitute"? How do you get one?
5. Why does the Church use candles in divine services? How many candles are used, and when?

Things to Do

1. Draw a picture of an altar with candles. Practice with a pencil and eraser "lighting" and "extinguishing" the candles you have drawn. Be careful not to use real candles or fire in your home. You may cause a serious accident with real fire.
2. Make a list of the other Catholic churches in your area.
3. Study the first part of the *Confiteor* well. The *Confiteor* is easily mixed up. So be careful.

Lesson 13...

The Altar Boy Is Neat

In the past lesson, we learned about promptness. Today we will discuss another very important quality of the altar boy—neatness. WITHOUT NEATNESS AND CLEANNESS, AN ALTAR BOY'S SERVICE IS NOT COMPLETE. An altar boy should always be neat, but when he serves, he must be especially neat. As people say, he must be immaculate or just as if he stepped out of a band box.

When you present yourself to serve, be certain that your face and hands are scrubbed clean—no high-water marks either. Brush your teeth, too. Your fingernails must be clipped and cleaned. Your hair must be cut and carefully combed. Your shoes must also be polished.

All this cannot be done in five minutes. Give yourself plenty of time to get ready. In fact, most of all this should be done the night before. Try to have a clean handkerchief in your pocket, too.

To be neat and clean, you must have the right kind of equipment. Every altar boy should have a hand and finger brush, a fingernail file, a good comb, and a good toothbrush. Sometimes, ordinary soap doesn't do a good job on the hands either. You will need some sort of stronger soap for removing stains and grease. Have a bar of stronger soap handy when the ordinary face soap doesn't do the job. Another point—always shine your shoes before you wash your hands; otherwise, you will have to wash them over again.

Before you leave the house, then, check on these points:

face ★ *hands* ★ *nails* ★ *teeth* ★ *hair* ★ *shoes*

Latin Department

Welcome! If you are ready, we can take the second section of the *Confiteor* today:

bay-ah'-toe Mee**-kah-ay'-l**ee **ark-ahn'-jay-lo/**
bay-ah'-toe Yo-ahn'-ee **Bop-t**ee**s'-tay/**
sonk'-tis ah-po'-sto-lis Pay'-tro et Pow'-lo/

Please notice that **Pow'** is pronounced as in the Indian word *pow-wow*. Keep reviewing the first section too.

Today's Rubrics

The hat that the priest uses in church is called a *biretta*. Can everyone say it? Most priests wear one that has three fins and a large fuzzy ball called a *pom-pom* on the top. A good altar boy always knows how to handle the biretta. Here are a few rules:

When you receive the biretta, you may take it any way you wish. When you present the biretta to the priest, however, hold it by the front fin. The idea is that the priest can take it by the middle fin. (You can tell the middle fin because the opposite side is flat.)

At the beginning of Mass, the biretta is received at the foot of the altar, a genuflection is made, and the biretta is taken to the *sedilia* (the altar bench).

During the Mass, when you accompany the priest to the sedilia, you pick up his biretta first. Then you help him get seated, being careful to put his chasuble over the back of the sedilia or in the slot if it has one. After the priest is seated, you give him his biretta. (Be sure he gets the middle fin.) After the priest puts on his biretta, you bow to the altar and then to him. After this, you sit with him. Remember when you sit there, keep your head erect and your hands fully extended, flat on top of your thighs.

When the priest rises, take his biretta, place it on the sedilia, and accompany him back to the altar.

At the end of Mass, the biretta is given to the priest as he leaves the altar. When you genuflect at the *Last Gospel*, you go to the sedilia, get the biretta, and give it to the priest when he comes to the floor. After he gets the biretta, all genuflect and proceed back to the sacristy.

Things to Know

1. When should an altar boy get ready to serve?
2. When is an altar boy's service not complete? Explain.
3. What are some of the things every altar boy should have to be neat?
4. What points should a server check before leaving the house? What is a "high-water mark"?
5. What is a "biretta"? How should the "biretta" be handled?

Things to Do

1. Practice giving and taking the "biretta" at home by using an old hat.
2. Ask your family to take you on a visit to some of the Catholic churches on the list that you made.
3. Keep spending your time on the *Confiteor*—it is very important.

Lesson 14 ...

The Altar Boy Should Be a Minuteman of His Parish

Do you remember reading about the minutemen in American History? They played a very important part in the war for our independence back in 1776. These patriots promised to spring into action against the British at a *minute's* notice—that's how they got their name. When Paul Revere spread the news that the British were coming, the minutemen dropped whatever they were doing and picked up their muskets, ready to fight. Their readiness to serve when they were needed did much to win our independence.

Every altar boy should be a minuteman in his parish. Just like the patriots of 1776, he should be ready to spring into action at a minute's notice. You will usually know your altar appointments well in advance so that you can plan on them. In fact, ask your mother to write your appointments on the kitchen calendar or in her reminder book when the serving schedule comes out. Thus, the whole family can help you to remember. Once in a while, you will be asked to serve on short notice for some sick boy or for some unscheduled Mass. When the time comes—be a minuteman. Don't be selfish. Don't think up all sorts of lame excuses. Hear the call of duty—spring to action—be ready to serve. WIN FOR YOURSELF THE REPUTATION OF NEVER REFUSING. Be a real altar boy—a minuteman of your parish.

Latin Department

How do you do? Are you ready to begin the third section of the *Confiteor*? Well, here it is. There are some hard words in it. So be careful.

ohm'-nee**-b**oo**s sonk'-tis/**
et tee**'-b**ee **pah'-tair**
kwee**'-ah pay-kah'-v**ee **n**ee**'-mis/**
ko-gee**-tot-s**ee**-o'-nay vair'-bo et o'-pair-ay/**
may'-ah koo**l'-pah/ may'-ah k**oo**l'-pah/**
may'-ah mahx'-ee**-mah k**oo**l'-pah/**

It would be well for you to remember that at the words **et t**ee**'-b**ee **pah'-tair** you turn toward the priest, since you are speaking to him. Then at the three **may'-ah k**oo**l'-pah**'s you strike your breast three times, as a sign of sorrow for your sins. To strike the breast properly, you place the left hand just below the breast and strike your breast with the right hand. The hand is not clenched but kept flat with the thumb in the palm. Do these things when you practice the Latin so that you will remember them.

Today's Rubrics

For some reason or other, changing the missal at Mass gives many boys trouble. It is really very simple if you remember a few rules.

The priest will signal you in some way to come and get the missal. In some places he extends his hand, in others he looks around. *Get the signal used in your parish straight.*

When the priest gives the signal, you say **Day′-o graht′-s**ee**-ahs** (Thanks be to God). Then go up and stand beside the priest, facing the altar with hands properly folded. When he leaves the missal, you step onto the *predella* (the altar platform), bow, and pick up the missal. Be sure that you have a good grip on the missal stand. Don't try to rush but move slowly. (If your cassock is too long, you will get into trouble here.) *Hold the missal out somewhat; by looking under it you can see where you are going.* You can't look over it.

In most parishes, the missal is changed in a V-shape movement. The altar boy goes down diagonally to the floor, genuflects, and goes up diagonally to the Gospel side. Here he places the missal on the *mensa* (altar table) and turns it toward the priest.

Several times during the year, the priest genuflects after the Epistle or during the Gospel. The servers genuflect with him at these times. The server on the step should be careful to genuflect properly on the step on which he is standing.

In the next lesson we shall speak about the cross that the servers makes at the reading of the Gospel.

Things to Know

1. Who were the "minutemen"? How can a server be a minuteman?
2. What kind of reputation does a first-class server have?
3. What are the "predella" and the "mensa"?
4. How do you strike your breast during the *Confiteor*? How do you genuflect while standing on a step?
5. When you change the missal, how should you hold it? Explain.

Things to Do

1. Practice changing the "missal" at home on a table with a large book.
2. When you next attend Mass, notice how the priest gives the signal to change the missal.
3. Keep going over the *Confiteor*. Practice and only practice makes perfect.

Lesson 15 …

The Altar Boy Is Truthful at All Times

One of the greatest gifts that God gave mankind is the gift of speech. Even the most gifted animal is not able to speak. In a way, speaking makes us like God. So, a human being should use his gift of speech to praise God and to speak the truth. When we tell the truth, what we *say* agrees with what we *think*. Truth should be a big thing in our lives. Lying is an easy way out and drags down the person who uses it. The devil is the father of lies—don't follow him. If you do something wrong, admit it like a man and take your punishment on the chin. Don't feel sorry for yourself. You have it coming. Tell the truth and everyone will admire you for it. No one trusts a liar.

Above all, don't get out of trouble by blaming someone else. Men don't lie and tell tales on each other to save themselves. Only cowards do that. If you are getting blamed for what someone else did, you can politely say that you didn't do it, but don't lie. If someone is getting blamed for a thing that you did, have the courage to stand up and take the blame yourself. Also, if you should ever find it necessary to disagree with someone older than yourself or someone in authority, *be certain* that you are right before you speak—nine times out of ten they are right. But if you find it necessary to disagree, say something like, "I beg your pardon, but that is not right," or "Excuse me, Father, but I didn't do that." WHEN YOU POLITELY DISAGREE, YOU GET A HEARING.

Latin Department

Hello. Well, we go into the fourth part of the *Confiteor* today. Are you being careful with the endings of all these Latin words? Remember, the endings are very important because they change the meanings of the words. Here is the fourth section of the *Confiteor*. Ready?

> *ee'*-**day-o** **pray'-kor/**
> **bay-ah'-tahm** **Mah-***ree***'-ahm** **sem'-pair**
> **v***ee***r'-g***ee***-nem/**
> **bay-ah'-t***oo***m** **M***ee***-kah-ay'-l***oo***m**
> **ark-ahn'-jay-l***oo***m/**

Even though the last part of the *Confiteor* is much like the first part, it is different just the same. You can easily mix up the same sounding words if you are not careful. Please be careful of your word endings. By the way, are you being careful of the accent marks, too?

Today's Rubrics

In the past lesson, you learned how to change the missal; today, we will go over the Gospel cross.

After the server has turned the missal toward the priest, he steps off the predella to the first altar step. He waits there with hands folded. When the priest comes to the missal he says *Dominus vobiscum* (The Lord be with you). The server answers **Et koom sp***ee***'-r***ee***-too too'-o** (And with thy spirit).

The priest then signs the missal and says *Sequentia Sancti Evangelii secundum Matthaeum,* or *Marcum,* or *Lucam,* or *Joannem* (Continuation of the Holy Gospel according to St. Matthew, or Mark, or Luke, or John). The server answers **Glow'-r**ee**-ah t**ee**'-b**ee **Daw'-m**ee**-nay** (Praise be to Thee, O Lord).

At the same time, the priest and server make the Gospel cross in this way:

1. Disjoin the hands. Place the left hand on the breast.

2. Keep the right hand extended *flat*.

3. Use the inside of the thumb (not the *side* but the *inside*) to make a *small* Sign of the Cross on the forehead, and the closed lips, and the breast.

4. When finished, rejoin the hands as before.

When the priest pronounces some form of the holy name of Jesus, make a head bow and return to your place. If, after a few lines, the holy name is not said, then return to your place but without a bow.

At the end of the Gospel (the priest usually kisses the missal), say this response: **Louse t*ee'*-b*ee* **Kr*ee'*-stay** (Praise be to Thee, O Christ).

Things to Know

1. What is truth? Why is truth a big thing in our lives?
2. If we must disagree with our superiors, how do we go about it?
3. What must we do if we are wrongly accused?
4. Name the four Evangelists (writers of the Gospels).
5. Why are the endings of Latin words so important?

Things to Do

1. Practice making the Gospel cross very carefully before your mirror at home.
2. Review the Sign of the Cross, the bows, and genuflections in Lessons 8 and 9.
3. Practice the fourth part of the *Confiteor* very carefully. Keep reviewing, too.

Lesson 16 ...

The Altar Boy Respects the Holy Name

A Catholic boy, especially an altar boy, should be known for his cleanness of speech. He should learn to say what he means without swearing or cursing. Some people think it's smart to use bad language. Well, it isn't. It only shows that those people are really dumb. Only smart people can express themselves with the right words at the right time. Only ignorant people have to swear to get the point across. Remember, slang is one thing, but swearing and cursing is quite another.

ABOVE ALL, THE CATHOLIC BOY SHOULD SHOW THE GREATEST RESPECT AND REVERENCE FOR THE HOLY NAME OF JESUS CHRIST. St. Paul tells us that at the name of Jesus, every knee should bend. For this reason, good Catholic boys always bow their head when they hear the holy name. Do you?

Never kick the holy name of God around like a football in your language. It is the most sacred of all words. You wouldn't spit on the crucifix certainly. So, never drag the name of Jesus Christ around in the dust of the streets. If you hear someone misuse our Lord's name, bow your head and say very quietly, "Blessed be the name of Jesus." In this way, you will be making up for the insult offered to our Lord. Sometimes we do not get very good example from grownups on this point. They should know better. Let's not listen to such bad example, but let's do what is right. After all, we must learn to stand on our own two feet. Maybe none of us are as good as we should be, but at least we can be loyal to our Lord's holy name.

Latin Department

Come in, boys. Here we are at the fifth and final section of the *Confiteor*. Let's go into the home stretch:

bay-ah'-too**m Yo-ahn'-em Bop-t**ee**s'-tahm/
sonk'-toes ah-po'-sto-loes Pay'-tr**oo**m et Pow'-l**oo**m/
om'-nes sonk'-toes et tay pah'-tair/
o-rah'-ray pro may ahd Daw'-m**ee**-n**oo**m
    Day'-**oo**m naw'-str**oo**m.**

Once again now, be careful of the endings and don't mix this part up with section two. Remember to turn toward the priest at **et tay pah'-tair**.

After the server finishes his *Confiteor*, the priest says two prayers. The server answers *Amen* after each prayer. These *Amens* should be *clear* and *firm*.

Today's Rubrics

The wine and water cruets are presented twice during Mass and the priest's hands are washed once. The first time you present the cruets is at the Offertory. This is called the first ablution. Here are some rules to remember (these are the directions to follow when you serve alone):

1. Remove the stoppers, if there are any, and place them on the credence.

2. Hold the wine cruet in the right hand—the handles

of both cruets turned toward the priest. Hold the cruets about the level of your chin—high enough for the priest to take it. Once the priest has taken the wine cruet, switch the water cruet to your right hand. You receive the wine cruet in your left hand. After the priest takes the water cruet, you switch the wine cruet back to your right hand. You then receive the water cruet with your left hand.

3. Strictly speaking, the cruets should be *lightly* kissed at the base of the handle as they are presented. The water cruet is kissed *after* it is blessed.

4. The priest pours enough wine for one mouthful and up to eight drops of water. For this reason, the cruets should not be filled to the brim—this makes them too difficult to use.

After the cruets are returned, the priest's hands are washed. This is called the *Lavabo*. In ancient times, the priest's hands would be soiled from receiving the gifts of the early Christians at this time in the Mass. Today, a collection of money is taken up instead of foodstuffs to help the parish carry on its work. But the priest still washes his hands to symbolize a spiritual cleansing.

When washing the priest's hands, hold the dish high enough so that the priest need not stoop over. Be careful to trickle the water and not dump it. The priest is also given a finger towel to wipe his hands. Sometimes the priests folds the towel before returning to the server; if not, the server should fold it before placing it on the credence table.

BY THE WAY, DO YOU USE YOUR SUNDAY ENVELOPES? It is very important that every member of the parish use the Sunday envelopes every Sunday.

Things to Know

1. Why do some people swear? What is one of the things a Catholic boy should be known for?
2. How should a Catholic boy treat the holy name?
3. What should we do if we hear our Lord's name taken in vain?
4. How much wine and water does the priest take at the first ablution?
5. Why is a collection taken up at Mass?

Things to Do

1. Practice using the "cruets" at home with old cups. Also practice washing the priest's hands. See if you can get someone to help you. Be sure to practice over the sink.
2. Check over your Sunday envelopes. Have you used them all to date?
3. Keep practicing the final section of the *Confiteor*. Pay close attention to the word endings. Remember how important the endings are.

Lesson 17...

The Altar Boy Loves Our Blessed Mother

An altar boy should be very devoted to the Blessed Virgin Mary. After all, we who wear the scapular of Our Lady of Mount Carmel are dedicated to her in a special way. She is our Mother and we should honor her in our daily life. Every altar boy should have a statue or a picture of the Blessed Mother in his bedroom. Every altar boy should have his own rosary. He should always carry it in his pocket, if not in his play trousers, at least in his school and dress-up ones. Did you know that you get a special blessing just for carrying your rosary with you? Well, you do. But no altar boy should be content just to carry his beads. He should say them as well. If possible, you should plan to say your rosary at least once a week in the church before the statue of our Blessed Mother.

Our Blessed Mother is a great lover of purity and she expects her altar boys to be very pure in their lives too. Certainly bad talk and bad books are out of the question for an altar boy. THE SERVER SHOULD SHOW EVERYONE IN HIS NEIGHBORHOOD HOW A BOY CAN BE A REGULAR FELLOW AND A PURE, REVERENT BOY AT THE SAME TIME. Our Blessed Mother will help you do this. So, be sure that you pray to her every day. She will help you be the kind of boy you want to be.

Latin Department

Come in, boys. Well, we are almost finished with the Prayers at the Foot of the Altar. This means we have seen most of the Latin. Isn't that good news? The Prayers at the Foot of the Altar end with four short responses to the priest's prayers. Watch them—they are tricky.

1. Et plebs t*oo*'-ah **lay-tah-b**ee'-t*oo*r **in tay.**
2. Et sah-loo-tah'-ray t*oo*'-*oo*m **dah no'-bis.**
3. Et klah'-mor may'-oo*s **ahd tay va'-n**ee-aht.**
4. Et koo*m **sp**ee'-ree-t*oo* t*oo*'-o.**

Keep going over your *Confiteor* and the other responses you have learned. Remember, you must repeat, repeat, repeat. See you next time.

Today's Rubrics

Important actions in the Mass are signaled by the ringing of the altar bell or hand bell. The altar boys

should know how to ring the bell. Even though the rules for ringing the bell at Mass differ from parish to parish, here are some rules to remember:

1. When you ring the bell, your ring should be firm and clear and not choppy.

2. Don't pick up the bell before it is time to ring it, otherwise, it will give off a tinkling sound.

3. Don't smother the bell by placing it down too quickly. Let the bell tone fade off before replacing the bell on the step.

After the *Gloria* of the Mass on Holy Thursday until the *Gloria* of the Mass on Holy Saturday, the altar bell is not used. Instead, the server uses a wooden clapper. In general, an altar bell is not used at Masses offered at the side altar. *First-class servers know how to ring the bell.*

Things to Know

1. How should an altar boy honor our Blessed Mother? Give examples.
2. What can you tell about an altar boy and his rosary?
3. Can you be pure and reverent and a regular fellow too? Explain.
4. What are three rules to remember in ringing the bell?
5. How do you learn your Latin responses?

Things to Do

1. Make certain you have a scapular or scapular medal to wear about your neck.
2. Keep going over the four Latin responses in this lesson.

Lesson 18...

The Altar Boy Receives Holy Communion Frequently

Holy Communion is the food of our souls. Just as your body needs good nourishing food to grow strong and healthy, you need Holy Communion to lead a good and holy life. No Catholic can really be good without going to Holy Communion often.

WHEN POSSIBLE, THE ALTAR BOY SHOULD RECEIVE HOLY COMMUNION WHENEVER HE SERVES. This is quite easy with the fasting rules we have now. The server should receive Holy Communion for three reasons:

1. He needs the help that our Lord gives in Holy Communion.

2. He takes a fuller and more active part in the Mass when he receives Holy Communion.
3. When the server receives Holy Communion, he also gives good example to the people.

The server should get ready to receive Holy Communion when he is scheduled to serve. If the server feels that he should go to confession, then he should take time and go. If you could not get to confession before Mass, do not be afraid to ask the priest to hear your confession when you meet him in the sacristy. This may take a little courage, but after all, we go to confession to tell our sins. You can't tell the priest anything new. The priest will think more of you for your honesty and courage, no matter what you confess to him. On the other hand, if you don't feel that you should go to Holy Communion, then *do not* receive Holy Communion. Don't care what anyone thinks— *never commit a sacrilege*. It doesn't make any difference if it's Midnight Mass and the church is packed. After all, it's a matter between God and yourself. Do your best to receive Holy Communion frequently though—you need it—everyone needs it.

Latin Department

Hello there! You should be happy to know that you are over the hardest part of the server's Latin by this time. The next responses are not so long or hard. Who remembers about the different kinds of *rites*? Well, even in the *Roman Rite* we have some *Greek*. The next response is the only Greek left in the Mass. Centuries ago there was much more. Who knows what it means?

Kee'-ree-ay   ay-lay'-ee-sawn (3 times).
Kree'-stay   ay-lay'-ee-sawn (3 times).
Kee'-ree-ay   ay-lay'-ee-sawn (3 times).

The server and the priest take turns saying these nine lines. Practice it the correct way with one another. One boy be the priest, and the others the servers. Try saying it in English with one another, too.

Today's Rubrics

Another important rubric for you to learn is how to assist at the Consecration. This is the way it is done in most parishes.

When the priest extends his hands over the chalice, the bell is rung once. The servers then go to the center, genuflect, and ascend to the *predella* (altar platform).

They then kneel to the right and the left side of the priest. The first server brings the altar bell with him. Each time the priest makes a genuflection, the servers make a deep bow. When the priest elevates the Sacred Host and Chalice, the servers lift the priest's chasuble slightly with the hand closest to the priest. Altogether, they bow four times, and lift the chasuble twice. It goes like this:

Bow—lift chasuble—bow
Bow—lift chasuble—bow

The first server rings the bell once at each genuflection and Elevation. It should go very smoothly. Be certain to let go of the chasuble when you make your bows. After the last bow, get up slowly, turn to the priest, come down to the floor, genuflect, and return to your places. During the Elevations, the servers should say *to themselves*, "My Lord and my God."

If the altar bell cannot be moved, the first server remains kneeling by the bell. The second server ascends to the *predella* for the Elevations, where he kneels to the left of the priest and lifts the chasuble with both hands. All else is the same.

Things to Know

1. What are the fasting rules for Holy Communion?
2. Why should the server receive Holy Communion at the Mass he serves?
3. What if the server is not in the state of grace?
4. What are "rubrics," "rite," "liturgy"?
5. Why is the Mass in Latin?

Things to Do

1. Practice assisting at the Elevations at home. Hang a towel on a chair or from the dresser drawer and pretend it is the priest's chasuble. Remember in all your practicing at home to be reverent. These are sacred actions.
2. Ask your parents about the old fasting rules. Who changed the rules and made it easier for us to receive Holy Communion more frequently?
3. Carefully practice the *Kyrie eleison*.

Lesson 19...

The Altar Boy Practices Catholic Action

Catholic Action is a word that has a lot of meanings, but for the altar boy it can have its own meaning. *Catholic Action* means doing good things to spread the cause of Christ on earth.

WITH HIS TRAINING AND HIS SKILL, THE ALTAR BOY CAN BE A GREAT FORCE FOR GOOD IN HIS PARISH—IF HE ISN'T SELFISH. In fact, there is always some good thing that he can do. When the altar boy is generous with his time and his energy for some good cause, he is practicing Catholic Action.

The altar boy can be a great help to the priest and the Sisters. He can help the old people, sick people, and poor people of his neighborhood. Emergencies come to every family and a lot of help is needed. If you know about an emergency, you should be Johnny-on-the-spot to offer your help. Just think of how many wonderful things that you can do for people who need your help. You can shovel snow, empty garbage cans, rake leaves, run errands, and any number of other things—all without seeking any pay or tips. How proud our Lord will be of you when you help people who need help.

Now, it is very possible that some people will take advantage of your goodness and ask you to help too often. If you are asked at a bad time, ask if you can do it later. If you feel that you are getting too much to do, speak to the priest about it and he will advise you what to do. But remember, our Lord loves the boy who isn't selfish with his time and energy. He is proud of the boy who practices Catholic Action. Look around you and see all the good you can do.

Latin Department

Come in. We are really getting there. Before long you will be finished. Today, we will do a little reviewing.

The priest says *Dominus vobiscum* many times in the Mass. As you know, it means "The Lord be with you." This is an ancient greeting of the early Christian days. It is always answered by **Et koom spee'-ree-too too'-o.** Actually, this means "And with thy spirit," but in everyday words, it means "May the Lord be with you, too."

Almost all the prayers in the Mass end with the same words. *Per omnia saecula saeculorum.* This means "forever" and refers to the fact that our Lord with the Father and the Holy Ghost rule forever. These words are always answered with a good loud clear *Amen*, which means "So be it."

In Lesson 14 we learned about the responses used at the changing of the book; perhaps we should review them in this lesson, too.

> **Day-o graht'-see-ahs.**
> **Glow'-ree-ah tee'-bee Daw'-mee-nay.**
> **Louse tee'-bee Kree'-stay.**

Today's Rubrics

Assisting the priest to distribute Holy Communion is a great privilege and an important responsibility. Make sure that you do it with the greatest reverence possible. Strictly speaking, the people should pass the paten for themselves; but for safety's sake, the altar boy usually does it for them. Here are ten rules for correctly assisting the priest. You should know these rules so well that the priest will never have to tell you what to do when the time comes to use them.

1. You are performing a most sacred duty. Never smile or recognize anyone you know at the Communion rail. Also, be very careful never to strike anyone in the throat with your paten through carelessness.

2. Hold the paten in the right hand extended—place the left hand on the breast as usual. Be careful to keep a proper distance from the priest. Never bump into him.

3. A paten, once used, must never be turned or drooped. It must be held perfectly level. A paten, once used, must not be set anywhere except on the corporal. Once used, a paten must always be purified (carefully cleared of all sacred particles).

4. If a Host or some small particle of a Host should fall on the paten—hold it perfectly level and the priest will remove the Host or else he will take the paten and tap it gently over the ciborium.

5. If a Host should fall on the floor or somewhere else, the priest will pick it up. But you should cover the exact spot immediately with some finger towel, or pall, or even a clean card. After Mass, the priest will wash the floor where the Host fell.

6. Sometimes, little children cause a problem, since there is no room between their chin and the railing for you to place the paten. Such children should be taught to stand at the Communion railing. If they remain kneeling, however, there is nothing for you to do but step back and wait for the priest to give Holy Communion unaided.

7. In going from one end of the Communion rail to the other, try to keep up with the priest. If he does not pause, however, you will not be able to assist

him with the first person. Don't try to leap into place—it can't be done. If he doesn't wait for you, it isn't your fault. So wait to assist with the second person.

8. Sometimes people, but mostly children, kneel with their hands by their mouth or under their chin. By *gentle* pressure of the paten, push their hands down.

9. After Holy Communion, the priest will take the paten from you and carry it to the altar to purify it. If the priest doesn't take the paten, however, then go up with him to the *predella* (altar platform) and place it on the corporal yourself.

10. The purified patens should be removed from the *mensa* (table) of the altar when the second wine and water is finished. Otherwise, you will have trouble replacing the missal.

Things to Know

1. What is Catholic Action? How can an altar boy practice Catholic Action?
2. What if some people ask you to do too much?
3. What should be an altar boy's attitude in helping the priest distribute Holy Communion?
4. If a paten is once used for Holy Communion, where is it placed?
5. What should the server do if a sacred Host falls on the floor?

Things to Do

1. Make a list of Catholic Action for use in your own neighborhood.
2. Be able to demonstrate the ten rules for assisting at Holy Communion.
3. Practice the Latin responses in this lesson used at the Epistle and Gospel. Review the "Gospel Cross" in Lesson 15.

Lesson 20...

The Altar Boy Is Precise

Precision, precision, precision—there is an important word. *Precision* means exactness. When you are given an assignment, you must carry it out exactly as it is given to you. You must be precise. Half-done assignments, poorly done assignments, misunderstood assignments, all mean the same thing—no *precision*.

Before you can be precise, you must first know *exactly* what is expected of you. When you are given directions, don't half-listen—give your full and complete attention. If you do not understand directions, ask that they be repeated or be put in simpler language. Sometimes, older people speak too fast or use words that you do not understand. If this happens, tell them. NEVER START ON AN ASSIGNMENT WHEN YOU DO NOT KNOW

WHAT YOU ARE DOING. If you do not understand the directions, ask that they be repeated. Even if they are repeated ten times and you do not understand them say, "I'm sorry, but I do not understand." If you are asked to deliver a message that you will not be able to remember, ask that it be written down. It doesn't make any difference if you are called a "dumbbell" or a "boob." If you don't understand the assignment, say so.

Once you are given an assignment and you fully understand it, then *do it in the way you are told to do it and not your own way.* Remember, *precision, precision, precision.* Here are a few examples to test your precision:

TELL THE LADY WITH THE PURPLE HAT IN THE THIRD ROW TO CLOSE THE WINDOW UNDER THE SECOND STATION OF THE CROSS.

Which lady? Where is she sitting? What is she supposed to do? Which window? Where is it located? Get the idea?

Here are some more:

GO TO THE SACRISTY AND GET ME THE TABERNACLE KEY IN THE THIRD DRAWER ON THE LEFT. IT IS IN A PINK BOX MARKED "KEYS." THE TABERNACLE KEY HAS THE LONGEST CHAIN ON IT OF ALL THE KEYS IN THE PINK BOX.

Go where? Why? What drawer? On the right or left? What color box? Which key? How do you know which key?

LIGHT THE SIX CANDLES ON THE LOWER GRADINE OF THE ALTAR, THEN EXTINGUISH THE

VIGIL LIGHTS IN FRONT OF THE STATUES. LEAVE THE VIGIL LIGHTS IN FRONT OF THE BLESSED VIRGIN'S STATUE LIGHTED.

How many candles? Where? What then? What vigil lights are left lighted?

Remember, get the message straight. Know what is expected of you and then do it with *precision, precision, precision.*

Latin Department

Well, boys, here we are. This is the last long response. If you get this one, you have it made. After you have presented the cruets for the first time and washed the priest's hands, you return to the center and kneel. The priest turns and says *Orate Fratres*—you answer:

S*oo*-sh*ee*'p*ee*-aht Daw'-m*ee*-n*oo*s sock-r*ee*-fee'-ch*ee*-*oo*m/ day mah'-n*ee*-b*oo*s t*oo*'-is/

ahd loud'-em et glow'-r*ee*-ahm naw'-m*ee*-nis
   s*oo*'-*ee*/

ahd *oo*-t*ee*-l*ee*-tah'-tem kwo'-kway naw'-strahm/
tote-s*ee*-*oo*s'-kway ay-clay'-z*ee*-ay s*oo*'-ay sonk'-tay.

There are some hard words in here but with practice you can do it. Remember, watch the endings.

Today's Rubrics

After the Communion, the cruets are presented again for the second ablution (washing). This time the servers do the pouring. Remember these six rules:

1. Hold the cruet as before—but this time by the handle. You do the pouring. Hold the cruet with your right hand. Your left hand is on your breast.

2. When the priest extends the chalice, pour the wine slowly until he raises the chalice as a signal for you to stop. Hold the cruet about an inch above the chalice to prevent hitting it. Then turn right and return to the top step of the predella. Turn and face the priest. Wait until he comes to the side for the washing of his fingers.

3. When the priest comes to the side, pour in only a little wine. He will signal when to stop pouring by raising the chalice slightly. Be careful not to touch his fingers with the cruet. Pour the water generously over his fingers, but do not dump it out all at once. Again, be careful not to touch his fingers

or bang the chalice with the cruet. (When serving alone, after pouring the wine, hang the wine cruet by the handle on the little finger of your left hand. Switch the water cruet to your right hand, and pour the water over the priest's fingers.)

4. Remember, when the priest has had enough wine or water, he will slightly raise the chalice—this is your signal to stop. Be alert and watch for it; if you don't see the signal, you will pour too much.

5. Remember to bow before and after presenting the cruets.

6. Remember to remove the purified patens from the mensa.

At the end of the Mass, the missal is changed again. In many parishes, the two boys who are serving change the chalice veil and missal together, after the second ablution. This is a difficult movement, so keep these points in mind:

1. After the second ablution, the servers go to the center and genuflect. Then each goes up to the predella the long way.

2. They bow together to the tabernacle—pick up the object—turn *toward the priest*—go down the short way and genuflect together.

3. Then each goes up the short way—the missal first. Each places the object down—they bow together to the tabernacle—*turn* to *the altar*—return the long way to the center—genuflect—return to their places.

When the book is replaced on the Epistle corner, it is not turned but is replaced as it was found earlier in the Mass—straight. This rubric requires a lot of practice to run smoothly.

Things to Know

1. What is "precision"? How can an altar boy practice it?
2. How should you carry out an assignment?
3. What if you don't understand an assignment?
4. Is there a difference in the position of the missal on the Gospel side from its position on the Epistle side? Explain.
5. How do you know when the priest has had a sufficient amount of wine and water?

Things to Do

1. Ask the family to test your precision by giving you complicated things to do and to remember. Show them the lesson for examples.
2. Be able to explain the five rules for the second ablution.
3. Study the **Soo-shee'pee-aht** by reading it over again and again.

Lesson 21 ...

The Altar Boy Is Reverent in the Sacristy and Sanctuary

An altar boy must realize that the sanctuary of his parish church is the most sacred place on earth for him. Each time he genuflects, it should be a real act of adoration to the Blessed Sacrament. The server's rubrics must be polished, his Latin perfect, and he must be neat and clean. The altar boy must be serious in his serving. He must be very devout and exact in the sanctuary.

It is very important to remember that silence and good behavior mast be the rule in the sacristy as well. Some altar boys who would never dream of acting up in the sanctuary are not so careful in the sacristy.

We all like to laugh and fool around. We wouldn't be human if we didn't, but, after all, there is a time and place for fooling and a time and place to be serious. We have said this before—it's a wise boy who knows the difference. It would be an awful mistake if any altar boy or group of altar boys thought that the sacristy were some sort of private playground.

Please remember, you are in the sacristy and sanctuary on business—the most serious business of all. You are there to worship and praise God. ANY ALTAR BOY WHO LACKS THE PROPER SPIRIT OF REVERENCE IN SACRED PLACES WILL BE DISMISSED.

Altar boys must also try their best to keep the sacristy in proper order. After Mass, the cards and missal should be removed from the mensa of the altar and the altar covering put on correctly. Cassocks and surplices should be carefully hung (not thrown) in their proper places. All drawers and cabinets should be shut. Altar boys should see to it that all lights are put out when they leave (unless someone else does this). THEY SHOULD ESPECIALLY CHECK TO SEE THAT THE CANDLES HAVE BEEN PUT OUT AND THAT NONE ARE LEFT BURNING. IF THE CENSER HAS BEEN USED, THEN CHECK TO BE SURE THE LIGHTED CHARCOAL HAS BEEN PUT OUT. Otherwise, a fire may start.

Before leaving the church, altar boys should always make a brief visit to the Blessed Sacrament. Do all these things and your service will be *complete*.

Latin Department

Hello, boys. It's a good thing you got over the *Suscipiat*. The most important part of the Mass is called the *Canon*. The *Canon* is introduced by the great prayer of praise, called the *Preface*. You will make these responses to the priest:

PRIEST	SERVER
Per omnia saecula saeculorum.	**Amen.**
Dominus vobiscum.	**Et koom spee'-ree-too too'-o.**
Sursum corda.	**Hah-bay'-moos ahd Daw'-mee-noom.**
Gratias agamus Domino Deo nostro.	**Deen'-yoom et yoo'-stoom est.**

It should be pointed out that sometimes servers do not make these responses and other short responses very well. ONE OF THE REASONS IS THAT SOME BOYS LET THEIR ATTENTION WANDER DURING MASS. Make sure that you pay strict attention and give each and every response in a good, brisk, and clear voice. You represent the people. Remember to articulate and project your voice.

Today's Rubrics

The general position of the server is kneeling. At certain times, however, he stands and even sits. His position differs in various Masses. Memorize these rubrics and you will know what to do.

1. Low Mass—Kneel all through the Mass. Stand only for the two Gospels. If there is a sermon, sit at the sedilia. Remember to stand facing the tabernacle during the reading of the English Gospel.

2. Requiem High Mass—In Masses offered in black and purple vestments, kneel all through Mass. Stand only at the two Gospels and the Preface. (Sit with the priest, if there is a Sequence.) To be very correct, however, in Masses offered in black or purple vestments, you should rise at *Dominus vobiscum* and kneel at the *Oremus* that immediately follows.

3. Festal High Mass —In all other sung Masses, stand each time the priest sings. Sit with the priest at the sedilia during the *Gloria* and *Credo*. Remain standing between the *Pater noster* and the *Pax Domini*. Kneel at all other times.

During the *Gloria* and *Credo*, the priest removes his biretta at certain sacred phrases. The servers should rise and bow to the priest at these phrases; turn to the altar as they are sung; and then, turning back to the priest, bow and be seated. These sacred phrases are:

Gloria

Ah-doe-rah′-moo**s tay**
Graht-see**′-ahs ah-g**ee**′-m**oo**s t**ee**′-b**ee
Yay′-soo **Kr**ee**′-stay**
Soo**′-sh**ee**-pay day-pray-kot′-s**ee**-o-nem naw′-stram**
In glow′-ree**-ah Day′-**ee
(return to altar)

Credo

Jay'-soo**m Kr**ee**'-st**oo**m**
See**'-m**oo**l ah-doe-rah'-t**oo**r**
Et in-car-nah'-too**s est . . .**
et ho'-mo fahk'-t**oo**s est (kneel for this)
Et *v*ee**'-tahm ven-t**oo**'-r**ee **say'-k**oo**l-**ee
(return to altar)

When sitting at any time, keep the hands flat on the thighs and the feet together.

Things to Know

1. What is required of an altar boy in the sanctuary? In the sacristy? Explain.
2. How can the sacristy be kept in good order? List the points to be watched.
3. What would be an awful mistake for any altar boy to make? Explain.
4. What points are especially important for a server to check? Why?
5. What makes an altar boy's service complete? Give examples.

Things to Do

1. Memorize the rules for rising, sitting, and kneeling at Low Mass, Requiem High Mass, Festal High Mass.
2. Review the material on rising, sitting, and kneeling in Lesson 10.
3. Study the responses used in the Preface. Very often altar boys have trouble remembering these responses. So, study them well.

Lesson 22...

The Altar Boy When Serving Is on Parade

A visitor to West Point recently was watching the cadets out playing different games. Dressed in their old clothes, they shouted and jumped and pushed one another around. It was a loud, laughing, and pretty dirty-faced bunch of boys that filed past him on the way back to the barracks.

Later, the visitor watched the same cadets on dress parade. What a difference! It was hard to believe that it was the same group of young men that he had seen in the morning. Each face was scrubbed clean. Each uniform was pressed and spotless. The highly polished brass glittered in the sun. In complete silence and absolute attention, the cadets marched in perfect formation. It was marvelous.

Why such a change in the same group of young men? Well, the first time they were at *play;* the second time, they were *on parade*. They knew the difference. Do you?

IT'S A SMART BOY WHO UNDERSTANDS THAT THERE ARE DIFFERENT WAYS TO ACT AT DIFFERENT TIMES. There is a time to talk and a time to be quiet. There is a time to play and a time to be serious. There is a time to *relax* and a time to be *on parade*.

When you serve, you are on parade just like the West Point cadets. Never make the mistake of thinking that you can dress and act as if you were out playing games. Never!!! You must have what we call *altar-presence*. Soldiers have what is called a military bearing—you must have *altar-presence*. When you get vested in cassock and surplice, you are in the uniform of the Church. You are God's honor guard on parade. Serve with *silence*, *correctness*, and *dignity*. Have your mind on your rubrics and your Latin. No fooling, no giggling, no careless serving—see that this is your rule. There is a big, a very big difference in playing and parading. See that you remember it when you serve. Have *altar-presence*. You are *on parade*.

Latin Department

My goodness, we are just about finished. Aren't we? Well, let's get busy. After the Canon, the priest begins the *Communion* with the Lord's Prayer or "Our Father." He ends with these words *Et ne nos inducas in tentationem*— (And lead us not into temptation). The server answers

Said l*ee'*-**bair-ah** **nos** **ah** **mah'-lo** (But deliver us from evil). The priest then adds the "Amen."

After this the priest breaks the large Host and dropping a Particle into the chalice he says:

PRIEST	SERVER
Per omnia saecula saeculorum.	**Amen**.
Pax Domini sit semper vobiscum (May the Peace of the Lord be always with you).	**Et k**oo**m sp**ee**'-r**ee**-t**oo **t**oo**'-o** (And with thy spirit).

These two responses just about finish things. Be certain that you are reviewing each day. Remember the first-class server recites his Latin correctly, clearly, and with certainty.

Today's Rubrics

Before we begin, let's review what we learned about candles in Lesson 12. The altar boy must exercise great care and attention with the candles. Here are a few general rules for you to keep in mind.

Candle Lighter

The candle lighter-extinguisher is carried in the right hand, with the left hand placed on the breast as usual. The lighter should be held in the middle of the pole at about a 50-degree angle (/). BE CAREFUL NOT TO BANG THE FLOOR WITH THE POLE WHEN YOU GENUFLECT.

102

Lighting the Candles

In lighting the candles, you must keep in mind not to drop sparks or grease on the altar cloth. REMEMBER, NEVER ADJUST THE LIGHTED TAPER OVER THE ALTAR CLOTH. Always adjust it over the predella. In that way, you can stamp on any sparks that drop.

To light the candles quickly and properly, you must keep a hook about one inch long on the burning end of the taper. Be certain to hold this flaming hook right into the brass follower on top of the candle. *The larger the candle—the longer it takes to light.* Hold the flame steady and keep the hook in the follower. The flaming taper must be pushed up and bent into a hook again and again, *but never over the altar cloth.* If a candle does not seem to light, step back and make sure that it isn't lighted. Try again and if it doesn't light then, it must be taken down and the candle wick pulled up. If you cannot do this, tell the priest.

Extinguishing the Candles

Remember, you extinguish the candles backward. What does that mean? Extinguish the candles slowly and carefully. Never blow them out. This spills or spatters the wax. Use the extinguisher. It is important to smother the flame. Don't mash out the flame. BE CAREFUL NOT TO SQUASH THE CANDLE WICKS—this makes the wicks hard to light again. After you extinguish one or two candles, smoke collects in the extinguisher and this helps to put out the flame more easily.

Care of the Lighters and Extinguishers

First-class servers always check the tapers before every service. If a taper looks too short to do the job, it should be replaced with a new taper. After the candles are lighted, the taper should be pulled into the tube and extinguished. HOWEVER, THE TAPER SHOULD THEN BE IMMEDIATELY PUSHED OUT OF THE TUBE. Otherwise, the warm taper will stick to the sides of the tube and jam. If through someone's carelessness, the taper becomes stuck in the tube, take a lighted taper and hold it, briefly, to the part of the tube where the taper is stuck. Then pull the taper down. When it comes loose, push it forward all the way out of the tube. Keep the taper out of the tube until it is cooled.

The bell-like part of the extinguisher also requires attention. It should be cleaned out after being used with a cloth or paper towel. This prevents grease and black wax from collecting in the bell. If grease collects in the extinguisher bell, it will drop in big black spots on the altar cloth when you are extinguishing candles.

A Word of Caution and Safety

You know what great care and attention that you must pay to this important job. You understand that it can be dangerous. Well, sometimes, no matter how careful you are, accidents are bound to happen. If your surplice should ever catch on fire, remember:

DO NOT RUN—DO NOT RUN—THIS WILL SPREAD THE FLAME.

Do not be afraid to shout for help if you catch on fire, even during services. Roll around on the floor until the flames are smothered—above all, don't run. IN EVERY SANCTUARY AND SACRISTY, THERE SHOULD BE A SMALL HAND FIRE EXTINGUISHER WHICH EVERY BOY THERE SHOULD BE TAUGHT TO USE. It is very important that you never play with this or any other fire extinguisher. What a terrible thing if a fire extinguisher would not work in time of fire because you played with it. What if some boy is burned badly or the church is greatly damaged because you were fooling with the extinguisher! Years can go by without any fire accidents, but they can happen—be prepared.

Things to Know

1. What did the visitor to West Point find there? What does this mean to a server?

2. What is one of the things a smart boy understands? Explain.
3. What is altar-presence? How should an altar boy serve?
4. What are some important things to remember about lighting candles?
5. How should you care for the lighter-extinguisher?

Things to Do

1. Talk over fire safety with your-parents. Explain to them what safety measures you have learned in this lesson.
2. Look around your school, church, and even your home. How many fire extinguishers do you find? Do you know how to use them? Perhaps some of you could call on your local fire department and ask for advice about fire safety.
3. You know the responses in this lesson already. Spend your time reviewing the ones you have trouble with.

Lesson 23...

The Altar Boy Holds Serving as
His First Loyalty

Remember the very first day you began to study
LEARNING TO SERVE? You were told that serving must
be your first loyalty. Now that you are just about finished
with the course, you should think about this a great
deal. When you become an altar boy, your duties as a
server come first—everything else comes second to it.
Serving must be your first loyalty. There is no reason at
all why you cannot be active in other things, too. Most
of the time, there should be no conflict. You should
never be put into a position where you have to choose
between loyalties. However, there are times when this
happens. You should get help at those times to make

the proper choice, but remember, serving is your first loyalty—it should come first. As you grow older, you will be active in many more things than you are now. You will want to do more things. Just remember where your first loyalty belongs. If any boy doesn't intend to make serving his first loyalty, he should not accept the cassock and surplice. History and literature are full of examples of great people who heard the call of duty and followed their first loyalty. They left everything else behind. WHEN THE TIME COMES FOR YOUR LOYALTY TO BE TESTED, REMEMBER WHERE IT BELONGS.

Latin Department

Well, come in for the last time. You certainly have learned a lot in the months that you have been dropping in here. Let's hope that you remember it. Are you ready for the very last responses? Here they are:

At the end of the Mass, the priest usually gives a blessing. Before the blessing, he turns to the people and says:

PRIEST	SERVER
Dominus vobiscum.	Et koom spee'-ree-too too'-o.
Ite, missa est (Go, the Mass is ended).	Day'-o graht'-see-ahs (Thanks be to God).

Around Easter two *Alleluias* (Praise the Lord) are added by the priest and the server:

PRIEST	SERVER
Ite, missa est. Alleluia, alleluia.	**Day'-o graht'-*see*-ahs. Ah-lay-l*oo*'-yah, ah-lay-l*oo*'-yah.**

After the priest gives the blessing, the server answers a good and clear *Amen*.

In Requiem Masses, the priest says *Requiescat in pace* (May he [or she] rest in peace). The server answers *Amen*.

If a procession is to follow the Mass, the priest does not say the *Ite, missa est* and does not give the blessing. Instead he says *Benedicamus Domino* (Let us bless the Lord). The server answers **Day'-o graht'-*see*-ahs.**

The Last Gospel on Palm Sunday is said only in Masses at which the palms are not blessed. In these Masses the Last Gospel is read from the missal and not the altar card. In these cases, the priest will give the regular signal as at the *Epistle*. The book is changed in the same way as before. The only difference is that the server waits at the foot of the altar with the missal. He kneels for the priest's blessing, answers *Amen*, and then goes up the short way with the missal, just as at the Gospel.

Today's Rubrics

The censer or thurible is used to give incense in solemn ceremonies, some blessings, and Benediction. The censer-bearer or thurifer carries the censer and incense boat (it was formerly shaped like a boat). Some servers never learn to handle the censer properly. Read over these rules and keep them in mind.

1. The censer is carried in the right hand with the arm extended out and with the elbow at the side. The incense boat is carried in the left hand, resting on the breast.

2. When genuflecting, be careful to lift the censer so as not to bang it on the floor.

3. Opening the censer is always a problem. There are many different kinds of censers. Each kind is opened differently. Learn how to open your parish censer quickly and correctly.

4. When presenting the open censer for incense, be certain to hold it high enough and close enough for the priest to reach it. The incense boat should be held right next to the open censer.

5. When incensing someone, bow before and after you incense. When bowing, the censer is held in the right hand; the left hand is on the breast.

6. To incense anyone or anything—place the top of the chain in your left hand and keep it on the breast. With your right hand, grasp the bottom of the chain near the censer. Now lift the censer to a height just below your eyes, then swing it toward the object or person in a double or single swing. Remember to lower the censer after each double or single swing. Be careful of the chains or you will get all tangled up.

7. In incensing, there are two kinds of swings—the double swing and the single swing. The double swing is given: swing, swing, down. The single swing is given: swing, down. The single and double swings may be given in sets of one, two, or three. Here are the swing patterns:

DOUBLE SWING:

3 doubles: swing, swing, down; swing, swing, down; swing, swing, down.

2 doubles: swing, swing, down; swing, swing, down.

1 double: swing, swing, down.

SINGLE SWING:

3 singles: swing, down; swing, down; swing, down.

2 singles: swing, down; swing, down.

1 single: swing, down.

Different objects and different officers in the Mass are incensed with different swings. When rehearsing for a service, you will be told what pattern to use. The main thing for you to do now is to learn how to give the different swings.

Along with learning to use the censer, you should learn how to light the charcoal. Remember, anything that requires fire is somewhat dangerous. So be careful. There are different kinds of charcoal. Each is lighted differently. You need experience to light the kind that is used in your parish.

To be most useful, the lighted charcoal should be a red-hot coal—not half-lighted. This means that the charcoal should be lighted at least fifteen minutes before it is to be used. BUT IF YOU HAVE BURNING CHARCOAL IN A CENSER, BE CAREFUL TO REMOVE THE TOP ON THE CENSER. Otherwise, it gets too hot to handle.

After the service, the charcoal should be carefully emptied from the censer in a safe place. Many sacristies have a pail with water for this purpose. If you are not careful when you empty out the charcoal, you may start a fire. SOMETIMES FIRES START IN CHURCHES AT NIGHT AFTER EVERYONE IS GONE BECAUSE SOME ALTAR BOY WAS CARELESS WITH LIGHTED CHARCOAL OR FAILED TO EXTINGUISH A CANDLE.

Things to Know

1. What is an altar boy's first loyalty? Explain.
2. How do different loyalties sometimes clash? Give examples.
3. How is the missal changed for the second time? What about the priest's blessing?
4. When is lighted charcoal most useful? Explain.
5. If you burn charcoal in the censer, what are some things to remember?

Things to Do

1. Make a censer at home out of a piece of rope and a coffee can. Be careful not to cut yourself on the can. Ask your mother to help you.
2. Practice your censer swings at home with your homemade censer. Do not make a fire in it.

3. Study the final responses in this lesson. Be certain to learn the different responses and when they are used. Remember to practice a good and clear *Amen* for the blessing.

Lesson 24...

The Altar Boy Knows the Mass

Every altar boy should know the various parts of the Mass. You probably know already that the Mass has two general divisions—the *Mass of the Catechumens* and the *Mass of the Faithful*. The first part is named after those who studied the catechism before they were baptized— the *catechumens*. The first part of the Mass acts as sort of a preparation for the second and more sacred part of the Mass.

Here are the parts of the Mass of the Catechumens. If you memorize these parts, you will be helped a great deal when you come to learn how to serve.

Mass of the Catechumens

1. *Prayers at the Foot of the Altar*—in which the priest and people admit their sinfulness. The *Confiteor* is the high point.
2. The *Introit*—this is the opening prayer of the Mass. It changes with the Mass.
3. The *Kyrie*—the ninefold prayer for mercy.
4. The *Gloria*—the prayer of praise—not said in every Mass.
5. The *Collect*—the special prayer of the day. It changes with the Mass. Sometimes there are other Collects called *Commemorations*.
6. The *Lesson*—a reading from the Old or New Testament,

usually taken from the Epistles. It changes with the Mass.

7. The *Gradual* and *Tract* or *Alleluia*—hymns sung as the book is changed from the Epistle to the Gospel side. These change with the Mass.

8. *Sequence*—a long prayer in verse form. There are five sequences. The sequence rarely appears in the Mass. The most common one is the *Dies Irae* which is found in the Requiem Mass.

9. *Gospel*—a reading from the life of Christ as written by one of the four Evangelists. It changes with the Mass.

10. *Sermon*—the sermon explains the Epistle and Gospel. It is not always given.

11. *Credo*—the *Credo* or Nicene Creed is a prayer of faith much like the Apostles' Creed. It does not appear in every Mass.

If you can memorize these parts, it will be a fine help to your serving. If you can explain the parts and understand them, it will greatly improve your knowledge of the Mass.

Mass of the Faithful

The second part of the Mass is called the Mass of the Faithful. It receives its name from the fact that in the early Church only the baptized or the "faithful" could remain for it. The catechumens had to leave. The early Christians attached a great air of mystery and secrecy to the Mass.

This second part of the Mass has four movements— (1) *Offertory*, (2) *Canon*, (3) *Communion*, and (4) *Postcommunion*.

1. In the *Offertory*, the priest takes bread and wine, blesses them, and offers them to God. The servers assist him by presenting wine and water and washing his hands.

2. In the *Canon*, the priest changes this blessed bread and wine into the Body and Blood of our Lord. The most sacred part of the Canon is called the *Consecration*. During the *Consecration*, the priest raises the Host and Chalice for all to see. This is called the *Elevation*.

3. In the *Communion*, the priest and people receive the Body and Blood of Christ, called the Holy Eucharist, as food for their souls.

4. In the *Postcommunion*, the priest and people give thanks to God for the blessings received at Mass.

If you have memorized the outline of the Mass of the Catechumens, and if you memorize this outline, you will know the whole framework of the Mass.

Another thing that you should remember is that some parts of the Mass never change—these parts are called the *Ordinary of the Mass*. Some parts change in every Mass—these parts are called the *Proper of the Mass*. Also, the Church Year has two Mass cycles: the Sunday Cycle and the Weekday Cycle or the Cycle of the Saints. The Sunday Cycle is divided into a number of seasons. These are: (a) Season of Advent, (b) Christmastide which includes the Season of Christmas and the Season of Epiphany; (c) Season of Septuagesima; (d) Lenten Season which includes the Season of Lent and Passiontide; (e) Paschaltide which includes the Easter Season, Ascensiontide, and the Octave of Pentecost; (f) Season per annum (throughout the year) which runs from January 14 to Septuagesima Sunday and from the first Sunday after Pentecost to Advent.

The Weekday or Saints' Cycle runs through the year. Weekdays are generally dedicated to feasts of our Lord, our Blessed Mother, the Apostles, and other saints.

Things to Know

1. What are the two general divisions of the Mass? How do they receive their names?
2. How many parts are there in the Mass of the Catechumens?
3. What are the four movements in the Mass of the Faithful?
4. What feast day is it today? What day is your patron saint's feast day?
5. What Sunday of the Church Year was last Sunday? What about next Sunday?

Things to Do

1. Be able to list all the parts of the Mass of the Catechumens and the Mass of the Faithful.
2. Name the seasons of the Church Year.
3. List some of the great feasts of the Church Year.

Lesson 25...

The Altar Boy Has a Knowledge of the Altar and Sacred Things

The altar is a symbol of Christ and on it the Holy Sacrifice of the Mass is offered. Your parish altar is a big thing in your life. An altar boy should know all about the altar and the sacred things around it.

The church building is divided into several parts. The largest is the *body of the church* or *nave* where the people sit. The part where the altar stands is called the *sanctuary*. It is separated from the body of the church by the *altar railing* and *altar gates*. The rooms or room off the sanctuary is called the *sacristy*. The area around the sanctuary inside the altar railing is called the *chancel*.

The altar must be of solid stone, usually marble. It must contain the relics of saints and martyrs in a small compartment called the *sepulcher*. The altar must be consecrated, usually by the bishop. It is marked with five crosses—one in the center and one on each comer.

There are different kinds of altars. There is the permanent altar made entirely of stone. In the United States, this kind of altar is rather rare. We use the portable altar—a small square consecrated stone usually set in a very large and highly decorated wooden or stone frame. We usually refer to the whole frame as the altar and the small consecrated stone as the *altar stone*. But it is important to remember that the so-called altar stone

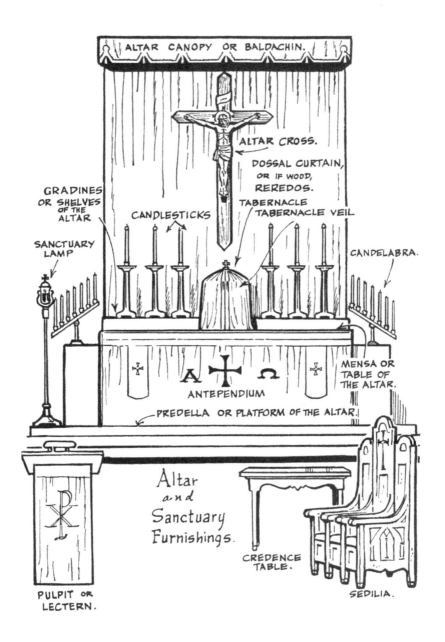

Altar and Sanctuary Furnishings.

- ALTAR CANOPY OR BALDACHIN.
- ALTAR CROSS.
- DOSSAL CURTAIN, OR IF WOOD, REREDOS.
- TABERNACLE
- TABERNACLE VEIL
- GRADINES OR SHELVES OF THE ALTAR
- CANDLESTICKS
- SANCTUARY LAMP
- CANDELABRA.
- MENSA OR TABLE OF THE ALTAR.
- ANTEPENDIUM
- PREDELLA OR PLATFORM OF THE ALTAR.
- PULPIT OR LECTERN.
- CREDENCE TABLE.
- SEDILIA.

is the real consecrated altar. All the rest, no matter how large, is only a frame.

The main altar is called the *high altar*. Other altars in the church are called *side altars*. As you look at the altar, the right side is called the *epistle side* and the left side the *gospel side*.

The high or main altar is usually set on a platform with three steps. The table part of the altar is called the *mensa*. The platform of the altar is called the *predella*. The sanctuary floor on which it all sets is generally referred to as *in plano*. The shelves very often found on the altar are called *gradines*.

A large canopy, called a *baldachin*, should hang over the altar. A *dossal curtain* often hangs from the canopy. If the background of the altar is carved wood or stone it is called a *reredos*. Every altar must have a crucifix which is called the *altar cross*.

In the United States, almost every high altar has a *tabernacle* in which the Blessed Sacrament is kept. The tabernacle is covered with a *tabernacle veil*. This is a sign that the Blessed Sacrament is present. The *sanctuary lamp* is also kept burning for the same purpose. The altar is covered with three *altar cloths*. The top cloth should reach the floor on either side of the altar. Many times the front of the altar is covered with a decorated cloth called an *antependium*, or frontal. The antependium and tabernacle veil are usually the color of the Mass being offered. When the altar is not in use for a number of hours, the mensa is covered with a cloth called the *altar cover* or *vesperale*.

The altar boy should also know by name all the sacred vestments, vessels, and furnishings, and be able to identify each.

Sacred Vestments

Amice	Cassock	Chasuble	Stole	Biretta
Alb	Cincture	Dalmatic	Tunic	Chalice veil
Burse	Maniple	Surplice	Cope	Humeral veil

Sacred Linens

Corporal	Pall	Ablution towel
Purificator	Altar cloths	Finger towel

Sacred Vessels

Chalice and paten	Pyx	Monstrance
Communion paten	Ciborium	Lunette

Sacred Furnishings

Candelabra	Altar cross	Altar cover
Altar cards	Antependium	Missal stand
Credence	Tabernacle veil	Lavabo dish
Vesting case	Holy-water	Cruets
Reliquaries	container	Censer and boat
Announcement	Holy-water	Missal
book	sprinkler	Processional
English Gospel	Ablution cup	cross
book	Ambry	Acolyte candles
Prie-dieu	Pulpit or lectern	Vesperale —
Sedilia	Altar benches	altar cover
Sanctuary lamp		

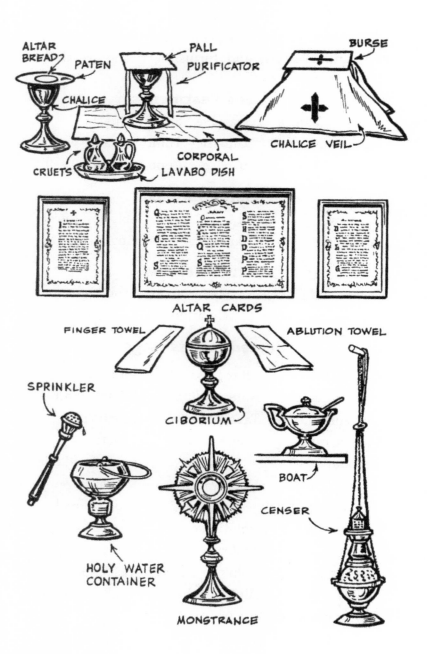

ALTAR BREAD · PATEN · PALL · PURIFICATOR · BURSE · CHALICE · CORPORAL · CHALICE VEIL · CRUETS · LAVABO DISH · ALTAR CARDS · FINGER TOWEL · ABLUTION TOWEL · SPRINKLER · CIBORIUM · BOAT · HOLY WATER CONTAINER · MONSTRANCE · CENSER

122

AMICE

ALB

CINCTURE

MANIPLE

STOLE

BIRETTA

CHASUBLE

123

Appendix

Prayers and Responses With Rubrics Added
Mass of the Catechumens

Prayers at the Foot of the Altar:

> (On several occasions during the year, the Prayers at the Foot of the Altar are omitted altogether. In Requiem Masses and Masses of Passiontide they arc shortened, going immediately from Introibo ad altare Dei to Adjutorium nostrum in nomine Domini.)

Priest: In nomine Patris, et Filii, et Spiritus Sancti. Amen. (The priest and the server make the Sign of the Cross together.)

Introibo ad altare Dei.

Server: **Ahd Day'-**oo**m kw**ee **lay-t**ee**'-fee-kaht/ y**oo**-ven-t**oo**'-tem may'-ahm.**

Priest: Judica me Deus et discerne causam meam de gente non sancta; ab homine iniquo et doloso erue me.

Server: **Kw**ee**'-ah t**oo **ez Day'-**oo**s/ for -t**ee**-t**oo**'-doe may'-ah/ kwah'-ray may ray-p**oo**l-is'-t**ee**/ et kwah'-ray tr**ee**s'-tis in-chay'-doe/ d**oo**m ah-fl**ee**'-ghit may in-**ee**-m**ee**'-k**oo**s.**

Priest: Emitte lucem tuam et veritatem tuam; ipsa me deduxerunt et adduxerunt in montem sanctum tuum et in tabernacula tua.

Server: **Et in-tro-*ee*'-bo ahd ahl-tah'-ray Day'-*ee*/ ahd Day'-*oo*m kw*ee* lay-t*ee*'-f*ee*-kaht / y*oo*-ven-t*oo*'-tem may'-ahm.**

Priest: Confitebor tibi in cithara, Deus, Deus meus; quare tristis es anima mea, et quare conturbas me?

Server: **Spay'-rah in Day'-o/
kwo'-n*ee*-ahm ahd'-h*oo*k cone-f*ee*-tay'-bor ill'-*ee*/
sah-l*oo*-tah'-ray v*oo*l'-t*oo*s may'-*ee* et Day'-*oo*s may'-*oo*s.**

Priest: Gloria Patri et Filio et Spiritui Sancto.
(*The priest and server make a deep bow together.*)

Server: **S*ee*'-k*oo*t ay'-raht in prin-ch*ee*'-p*ee*-o/
et n*oo*nk et sem'-pair/
et in say'-k*oo*-lah say-k*oo*-lo'-r*oo*m. Amen.**

Priest: Introibo ad altare Dei.

Server: **Ahd Day'-*oo*m kw*ee* lay-t*ee*'-f*ee*-kaht/ y*oo*-ven-t*oo*'-tem may'-ahm.**

Priest: Adjutorium nostrum in nomine Domini.
(*The priest and the server make the Sign of the Cross together.*)

Server: **Kw*ee* fay'-chit chay'-l*oo*m et tair'-ahm.**

Priest: Confiteor Deo, etc.
(*The priest makes a deep bow and prays the* Confiteor.)
...Orare pro me ad Dominum Deum nostrum.

Server: (*The server makes a shoulder bow, and turning toward the priest prays:*)

Mee-say-ray-ah'-toor too'-ee
  ohm-nee'-po-tens Day'-oos/
et dee-mee'-sis pay-kah'-tis too'-is/
pair-doo'-kaht tay/
odd vee'-tahm ay-tair'-nahm.

Priest: Amen.

Server: (*The server now turns straight ahead and making a deep bow prays:*)

Cone-fee'-tay-or Day'-o ohm-nee-po-ten'-tee/
bay-ah'-tay Mah-ree'-ay sem-pair
  veer'-gee-nee/
bay-ah'-toe Mee-kah-ay'-lee ark-ahn'-jay-lo/
bay-ah'-toe Yo-ahn'-ee Bop-tees'-tay/
sonk'-tis ah-po'-sto-lis Pay'-tro et Pow'-lo/
ohm'-nee-boos sonk'-tis/
et tee'-bee pah'-tair (*turning to the priest*)
kwee'-ah pay-kah'-vee nee'-mis/
ko-gee-tot-see-o'-nay vair'-bo et
  o'-pair-ay/
may'-ah kool'-pah/ (*Striking the breast three*
may'-ah kool'-pah/   *times*)
may'-ah mahx'-ee-mah kool'-pah/
ee'-day-o pray'-kor/
bay-ah'-tahm Mah-ree'-ahm sem'-pair
  veer'-gee-nem/
bay-ah'-toom Mee-kah-ay'-loom
  ark-ahn'-jay-loom/
bay-ah'-toom Yo-ahn'-em Bop-tees'-tahm/

sonk'-toes ah-po'-sto-loes Pay'-troo**m et
Pow'-l**oo**m/
om'-nes sonk'-toes et tay pah'-tair**
(turn to the priest)
o-rah'-ray pro may ahd Daw'-mee**-n**oo**m
Day'-**oo**m naw'-str**oo**m.**
(The server remains bowing deeply.)

Priest: Misereatur vestri omnipotens Deus et dimissis peccatis vestris, perducat vos ad vitam aeternam.

Server: **Amen.**

Priest: Indulgentiam absolutionem et remissionem peccatorum nostrorum, tribuat nobis omnipotens et misericors Dominus.
(During this prayer, the server returns from his deep bow and kneeling in a straight position makes the Sign of the Cross with the priest.)

Server: **Amen.**
(The priest and server now make a shoulder bow during the following responses.)

Priest: Deus tu conversus vivificabis nos.

Server: **Et plebs t**oo**'-ah lay-tah'-b**ee**-t**oo**r in tay.**

Priest: Ostende nobis Domine misericordiam tuam.

Server: **Et sah-l**oo**-tah'-ray t**oo**'-**oo**m dah no'-bis.**

Priest: Domine exaudi orationem meam.

Server: **Et klah'-mor may'-**oo**s ahd tay
vay'-n**ee**-aht.**

Priest: Dominus vobiscum.

Server: **Et k**oo**m spe'-r**ee**-t**oo **t**oo**'-o.**

127

Priest: Oremus.

(When the priest says Oremus, *both he and the server straighten from the shoulder bow. The priest ascends the altar steps and the server goes to his place. The priest kisses the place of the altar relics and goes to the Epistle side where lie reads the* Introit *from the missal. After this, he returns to the middle of the altar for the* Kyrie.)

Priest: Kyrie eleison.

Server: **K*ee*'-*r*ee-ay ay-lay-*ee*-sawn.**

Priest: Kyrie eleison.   Priest:

Server: **K*r*ee'-stay ay-lay'-*ee*-sawn.**

Priest: Christe eleison.

Server: **K*r*ee'-stay ay-lay'-*ee*-sawn.**

Priest: Kyrie eleison.

Server: **K*ee*'-*r*ee-ay ay-lay-*ee*-sawn.**

Priest: Kyrie eleison.

(The priest now recites the Gloria *in excelsis Deo, if there is one in the Mass. In sung Masses, the priest and servers usually sit at the sedilia while the choir sings the* Gloria. *After this, kissing the altar, he recites the* Collect.)

Priest: Dominus vobiscum.

Server: **Et k*oo*m sp*e*'-*r*ee-t*oo* t*oo*'-o.**

Priest: Oremus.

(The priest now recites the Collect.)

...Per omnia saecula saeculorum.

Server: Amen.

(If there are Commemorations, the priest begins them and ends them in the same way as the Collect. *The server answers—***Amen**.)

Priest: (The priest now reads the Lesson, or Epistle. At the end of the Lesson, or Epistle, he extends his hand.)

Server: **Day'-o graht'-see-ahs.**
(*The priest now reads the* Gradual *and* Tract *or* Alleluia. *The server comes to the missal to change it to the Gospel side of the altar. At a high Mass, if there is a* Sequence, *the priest and the server usually sit at the sedilia until it is finished before the missal is changed. On ember days and several other days, there is mere than one lesson. The server answers* **Day-o graht'-see-ahs** *at the end of each lesson, but changes the missal only at the end of the last lesson. The priest should arrange some special signal for the last lesson.*)

Priest: (*The priest now pauses in the center of the altar and prays before he reads the* Gospel. *After this, he goes to the side of the altar where the missal has been placed and begins the* Gospel.)
Dominus vobiscum.

Server: **Et koom spe'-ree-too too'-o.**

Priest: Sequentia Sancti Evangelii secundum (Matthaeum, Marcum, Lucam, or Joannem).
(*The priest and server make the Gospel cross together.*)

Server: **Glow'-ree-ah tee'-bee Daw'-mee-nay.**
(*At the end of the* Gospel, *the priest usually kisses the missal. The server answers.*)
Louse tee'-bee Kree'-stay.
(*The priest returns to the middle of the altar. If there is a sermon, it is given at this point. Otherwise, the priest recites the* Credo in unum Deum. *During the* Credo, *the server genuflects with the priest at the words—*Et incarnatus est. *The servers genuflect with the priest. In*

a sung Mass, the priest and servers sit at the sedilia while the Choir sings the Credo. *The servers kneel at the* Et Incarnatus Est. *After the* Credo, *or if there is no* Credo, *the priest again kisses the altar and turns to the people.)*

Priest: Dominus vobiscum.

Server: **Et koom spe'-ree-too too'-o.**

Priest: Oremus.

Mass of the Faithful

Offertory:

(*The priest reads the* Offertory *verse. After this he uncovers the chalice. The server goes for the wine and water. The priest offers the bread. Then taking the chalice to the Epistle side, he pours in wine and water. As the priest offers the chalice, the server prepares to wash the priest's hands. As the server washes his hands, the priest recites the* Lavabo. *After this both the priest and server return to the center of the altar for the* Orate Fratres.)

Priest: Orate Fratres, etc.

Server: **Soo-shee'-pee-aht Daw'-mee-noos**
    sock-ree-fee'-chee-oom/
    day mah'-nee-boos too'-is/
    ahd loud'-em et glow'-ree-ahm
    naw'-mee-nis soo'-ee/
    ahd oo-tee-lee-tah'-tem kwo'-kway
    naw'-strahm/
    tote-see-oos'-kway ay-clay'-zee-ay soo'-ay
    sonk'-tay.

Priest: Amen.
    (*The priest reads the* Secret *prayer and then begins the* Preface.)

...Per omnia saecula saeculorum.

Server: **Amen**.

Priest: Dominus vobiscum.

Server: **Et koom spee'-ree-too too'-o.**

Priest: Sursum corda.

Server: **Hah-bay'-moos ahd Daw'-mee-noom.**

Priest: Gratias agamus Domino Deo nostro.

Server: **Deen'-yoom et yoo'-stoom est.**
(*The priest sings or reads the* Preface *which ends with the* Sanctus *and* Benedictus. *The priest then begins the* Canon *of the Mass.*)

Canon:

(*During the* Canon, *the server makes no responses but assists during the* Elevation of the Host and Chalice.)

Communion:

(*The* Communion *of the Mass begins with the* Pater noster.)

Priest: Per omnia saeeula saeculorum.

Server: **Amen**.

Priest: Oremus. . . . Et ne nos inducas in tentationem.

Server: **Said lee'-bair-ah nos ah mah'-lo.**

Priest: (*The priest then breaks the Host and prays:*)
Per omnia saeeula saeculorum.

Server: **Amen**.

Priest: Pax Domini sit semper vobiscum.

Server: **Et koom sp**ee'**-r**ee**-t**oo **t**oo'**-o.**

(*The priest then recites the* Agnus Dei, *the three prayers before Communion and the* Domine non sum dignus. *At this time the server goes for the Communion paten and returns. The priest raises the small Host to the people and prays the* Domine non sum dignus *three times. After this, he distributes Holy Communion with the aid of the server. After Communion, the server gives the priest the Communion paten, and goes for the wine and water. After the priest has taken the* second ablution, *the server changes the missal, and sometimes the veil. He then returns to his place.*)

Postcommunion:

(*The priest now reads the Communion prayer. This is followed by the Postcommunion prayer and any Commemorations to be made.*)

Priest: Dominus vobiscum.

Server: **Et koom sp**ee'**-r**ee**-t**oo **t**oo'**-o.**

Priest: Oremus. . . . Per omnia saeeula saeculorum.

Server: **Amen**.

Priest: Dominus vobiscum.

Server: **Et koom sp**ee'**-r**ee**-t**oo **t**oo'**-o.**

Priest: (*Having come to the middle of the altar, the priest now dismisses the congregation. This prayer may differ from Mass to Mass. The server should be careful to give the correct response.*)

    1. Ite, missa est.

    2. Requiescant in pace.

    3. Ite, missa est, alleluia, alleluia.

    4. Benedicamus Domino.

Server: 1. **Day'-o graht'-s**ee**-ahs.**

2. **Amen**.

3. **Day'-o graht'-s**ee**-ahs ah-lay-l**oo**'-yah ah-lay-l**oo**'-yah.**

4. **Day'-o graht'-s**ee**-ahs.**

Priest: (*In most Masses, except Requiem Masses, the priest gives a blessing.*)

Benedicat vos omnipotens Deus, Pater, et Filius, et Spiritus Sanctus.

Server: **Amen**.

(*On Palm Sunday, the missal is changed again for a second time to the Gospel side. The server makes the changes after the* Postcommunion prayer *in the usual way.* However, he waits at the bottom of the steps where he kneels, for the blessing before taking the missal to its place on the Gospel side.)

Priest: (*The priest begins the* Last Gospel *or the special* Gospel *of the day if the missal has been moved for a second time.*)

Dominus vobiscum.

Server: **Et k**oo**m sp**ee**'-r**ee**-t**oo **t**oo**'-o.**

Priest: (*Once again, the priest and the server make the Gospel cross together.*)

Initium Sancti Evangelii secundum Joannem.

Priest: (*The priest reads the* Last Gospel. *When he has finished, the server answers:*)

Server: **Day'-o graht'-s**ee**-ahs.**

(*Several times during the year the Last Gospel is omitted altogether.*)

Check List for the Server Before Mass

Before Mass, cheek these points to make certain each is done:

- altar uncovered
- altar cards set up in correct position
- missal in place—open side to tabernacle
- both cruets filled on credence
- Lavabo dish and towel on credence
- Communion paten and bell in place
- altar book or card in place
- candles lighted—proper number

Some General Rules

No matter how complicated a ceremony becomes, it is still built upon simple rules. If you know these simple rules *by heart*, it will help you greatly in any ceremony at all.

1. In serving, all actions are performed slowly and smoothly and as noiselessly as possible.

2. In serving, one action is always fully completed before a second action is begun. Rising, sitting, and kneeling are three separate movements.

3. In serving, always move forward. Never walk sideways or backward. Never pop up or down. Never slide into a kneeling position.

4. In serving, the eyes are always lowered. Never stare into the congregation or gaze absently around the altar.

5. In serving, partners must perform all actions together. When turning, they turn toward each other. Groups of servers must be very careful to perform their actions smoothly and together.

6. In picking up objects, bow before you pick it up and bow after you put it down. Objects are generally presented with the right hand and received with the right hand.

7. Unless being used, the hands are always properly folded. In serving, when one hand is occupied, the other hand is always on the breast. When seated, the hands are extended flat on top of the thighs.

How to Carry Objects

From time to time you will be called upon to carry the acolyte candles, torches, the processional cross, and holy-water bucket. Here are a few tips for each one:

Acolyte Candles

The candle carried by the acolyte is the symbol of Christ—the Light of the World. Therefore, the acolyte candle should be held high, firm, and erect. Be careful not to tip it or hold it crooked. If you do, wax will drop on the floor and on your cassock. In holding the candlestick, place your outside hand (the farthest from your partner) high on the shaft of the candlestick. Place the inside hand on the base of the candlestick, grasping the bottom. When the acolytes accompany the cross with their candles, they do not genuflect; otherwise, they do genuflect.

Torches

In solemn ceremonies there are torchbearers. The server should carry the torch in his outside hand. He must be careful not to wobble it and not to bang it on the floor when he genuflects. All the torches should be held at the same height and perfectly straight.

Processional Cross

The processional cross is the sign of our salvation and should be held aloft proudly. Place both hands on the shaft of the cross. Place the right hand high on the shaft and the left hand lower on the shaft. Keep the figure of our Lord facing forward. If you hold the cross out from you a little bit, you will not kick it or bump it as you walk. Carry the cross slowly and with great dignity.

Holy-Water Bucket

The holy-water bucket is carried in the right hand with the left hand on the breast. Be careful not to spill the holy water. Present the sprinkler to the priest with your left hand. Be careful not to let the bucket hang carelessly.

Missal to the Altar

In some parishes the server carries the missal to the altar before the priest. The server should be careful to carry it resting against his breast with both hands supporting the underside. The open side of the missal should be to the altar boy's left. When placed on the altar, the open side always faces the cross.

Censer and Boat

See pages 109-112.

Ringing of the Bell

While the bell is rung in each parish according to custom, usually it is rung six times during the Mass. Here we distinguish between long and short rings. This difference is not mentioned in the rubrics, but it seems proper. If you can memorize the rules that follow, they will help you greatly:

1. When the priest uncovers the chalice—1 long ring
2. When the priest says *Sanctns, Sanctus, Sanctus*—3 long rings
3. When he *extends* his hands over the chalice—1 long ring
4. At the elevation—1 short ring for each genuflection and 1 long ring for each elevation
5. At *Domine non sum dignus*—3 long rings (if Holy Communion is to be distributed)
6. When the priest holds up the host before Communion—3 short rings (one at each *Domine non sum dignus*)

Please note number 5—it is easy to get mixed up. Remember the priest says *Domine non sum dignus* and not *Agnus Dei* when you ring. Please note: the bell is rung here only if Holy Communion is to be distributed.

The Kiss of Peace (Pax)

One of the very ancient and beautiful rubrics is the

kiss of peace in which those on ceremonies embrace one another. This is done to show how Christians should love one another, as our Lord commanded us to do. Here is how the *Pax* is given:

1. Turn toward one another.
2. The one who is receiving the *Pax* bows.
3. The one who is giving the *Pax* then places his hands on the shoulders of the one receiving; the one receiving places his hands under the elbows of the one giving the *Pax*. In this position they both embrace—each one inclining to the left shoulder of the other.
4. The one giving the *Pax* says: **Pahx tay'-koom**; the one receiving answers: **Et koom spee'-ree-too too-o**.
5. After this, they both separate, bow, and turn away back to their positions.
6. The *Pax* is passed from one end of the line to the next.

In Choro

In more solemn ceremonies a group of vested altar boys assist to add dignity and beauty to the service. We say these boys are *in choro*. The one who leads them is called the *Magister Chori* or 3rd Master of Ceremonies.

Boys *in choro* usually enter in procession, sit in a group, and receive Holy Communion in a body. Keep these points in mind:

When walking in procession remember that you are *on parade*. Your main duty is to look dignified and prayerful and to add beauty to the ceremony. Be certain to walk with head erect but eyes cast down, and hands properly joined. Always walk evenly with your own partner and keep directly in back of the boy ahead of you. All genuflections are made to the signal of the *Magister Chori*, who also signals all other changes in position. When assisting, be careful not to slouch or grow careless, but rise, stand, and sit as you have been instructed.

At Holy Communion time, those *in choro* receive in a body. Observe these directions:

1. When the *Magister Chori* signals—all stand and go into the aisle in rows four abreast.
2. At the signal all kneel for the *Confiteor*.
3. After the priest presents the Sacred Host three times, all rise.
4. Each row then advances in its turn to the bottom step, genuflects, and ascends to the predella where all kneel.
5. The Communion paten is passed from one to the other.
6. After the last boy in each row has returned the paten to the priest, all rise—turn left and go down to the floor—then turn right, back facing the priest, all genuflect and return to the pews. The two *middle* boys in each row lead back to the pews.

This skill takes some time to master, because some boys always want to turn the wrong way. However, practice until you can all do it perfectly.

Serving Mass at a Side Altar

From time to time, you will be asked to serve Mass at the side altar. Most of the time, this will be a last-minute arrangement. Here are ten points to remember:

1. Side altars do not always permit complete freedom of movement. Therefore, the server must sometimes abbreviate his method of serving.

2. The server must make the altar ready for Mass by first removing all flowers and decorations from the *mensa* (table) of the side altar. Remove the *vesperale* as well (altar covering placed over the altar cloths).

3. Stand the three altar cards on the *mensa*. The large card is placed in the center; the other two on the sides. The card whose first word is LAVABO is placed on the Epistle corner. The card whose first word is INITIUM is placed on the Gospel side.

4. Place the missal and stand on the Epistle corner of the *mensa*, with the open side of the missal facing the cross.

5. Place the filled cruets (be sure the water cruet is filled), the Lavabo dish and a finger towel on the credence. If there is no credence at the side altar, then use some flat but sturdy surface on the Epistle side. If this is not possible, then place the cruets, etc., on the gradine (shelf of the altar), or as a last resort on the *mensa* itself, but behind the missal if possible.

6. Be certain to have a card or a book available containing the prayers to be said after a low Mass.

7. If you wish to receive Holy Communion at the side altar Mass, tell the priest. He will consecrate a small host for you at Mass. In this case, place a Communion paten on the credence you have prepared.

8. After all is done, light the candles on the side altar (light the proper number) and return to the sacristy. If there is a light over the side altar, turn it on. If you do not know where the switch is, tell the priest.

9. If the quarters are cramped at the side altar, do your best to stay out of the priest's way. You must serve as well as you can under the circumstances.

10. During the Mass, keep the following points in mind:

a) Only the missal is changed. When you serve alone, the veil is not changed.

b) The bell is not used at the side altar during 40 Hours' Devotion or when Mass is being offered at the main altar.

c) At the *Lavabo*, open the towel and place it on your left arm for use of the priest.

d) At the Consecration, kneel on the top step at the celebrant's right and assist at the Elevations.

Holy Communion Outside of Mass

Whenever Holy Communion is given outside of Mass, the following points should be kept in mind:

1. The altar cover should be removed and two candles should be lighted on either side of the tabernacle.

2. The Communion paten should be placed on the credence. Check to see that the ablution cup and ablution towel is next to the tabernacle.

3. The server accompanies the priest to the foot of the altar where both genuflect. If the priest wears a biretta, the server places it on the altar steps.

4. When the priest goes up to the predella, the server goes to the side and recites the *Confiteor* adding the two *Amens* that always follow.

5. The server then assists the priest to distribute Holy Communion in the usual manner.

6. The server gives the priest the used paten or returns it himself to the corporal.

7. The server kneels on the bottom step for the priest's blessing.

8. The priest and server then return to the sacristy in the usual way.

9. The server extinguishes the candles, returns the paten to its proper place and covers the altar or arranges it for Mass, as he is instructed.

Asperges

The parish high Mass on Sunday should begin with a ceremony called the *Asperges* in which the celebrant of the Mass sprinkles the people with holy water. While a very simple ceremony, servers sometimes get mixed up in the *Asperges*. Here are a few rules to remember:

1. In the sacristy stand on either side of the priest if he blesses the holy water. Assist the priest as he puts on the cope. The altar gates should be opened.

2. Proceed to the altar in the usual way. The gospel-side server acts as holy-water bearer. When all three reach the foot of the altar, the epistle-side server takes the priest's biretta. All genuflect and kneel. The biretta is placed on the altar step by the server who opens the altar book to the *Asperges* ceremony. The holy-water bearer hands the priest the sprinkler.

3. The priest then rises to sing *Asperges Me* (*Vidi Aquam* in the Paschal season) but the servers remain kneeling. The priest then sprinkles the altar, himself, and then the two servers who bless themselves. The servers then rise and genuflect with the priest. All turn to the people. The servers are careful to turn toward the priest. As the priest leaves the sanctuary, the servers on either side hold the edges of the cope back to give the priest freedom of movement. The cope edge is held with the inside hand; the outside hand is placed on the

breast as usual. In larger churches, the gospel-side server should take the holy-water container with him since the priest may wish to dip the sprinkler in it again.

4. The priest and servers walk slowly down the aisle together, unless the aisle is small. Then the servers, still holding the cope, walk a little behind the priest. The priest sprinkles the people on both sides. As the choir sings *Gloria Patri*, the servers release the cope edges and turn with the priest to the altar and bow as deeply as he does. After this all turn and resume the sprinkling, the servers taking again the cope edges.

5. At the end of the aisle, the servers release the cope edges and all turn. The servers are careful to turn toward the priest. All then return to the altar. The servers still hold the cope edges as before.

6. At the foot of the altar all genuflect. The epistle-side server presents the altar book, or card, to the priest who then sings the prayer or oration. After this, the server returns the book, or card, to the altar step and all genuflect. The priest is given the biretta in the usual way. All then proceed to the sedilia or return to the sacristy where the servers help the priest to vest for Mass. The altar gates should be closed for Mass.

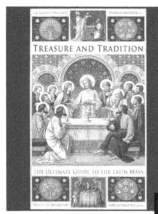

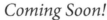

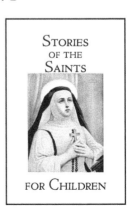

CPSIA information can be obtained
at www.ICGtesting.com
Printed in the USA
FFHW021807111019
55484252-61305FF